WOODEN BOATS

WOODEN BOATS

The Art of Loving and
Caring for Wooden Boats

Text by Andreas af Malmborg
Photography by Ola Husberg

Skyhorse Publishing

We wanted to write a book about wooden boats because we both grew up with wooden boats and feel we have some insight into their special qualities. When you've slept under the foredeck and listened to the water lapping against the planking… when you've heard the rigging creaking and felt the scent of varnish and paint… when you've swung open the cabin doors to be struck by a clear July morning filled with summer-dry mahogany and a hint of gasoline… when you've spent a January evening under a cover whistling to yourself with a can of linseed oil in your hand… when the temperature is only 10°F outside and your breath rises in a plume… then you've felt something of the uniqueness of wooden boats.

This book is about pleasure boats made from wood. We've tried to describe what makes them beautiful, fun, enchanting, practical, and special. Wooden boats demand a lot of work from you but they also reward you in return. A well-cared-for wooden boat gives its owner pride, confidence, and a special status. The preparatory work routines, the feeling of togetherness, the imagination and creativity released—it's all part of the great wooden boat experience. No country has a greater wealth of unique wooden boats than Sweden. In the pages that follow, we present a few of them.

We extend our thanks to all the professionals and owners who have given us their time, knowledge, and commitment, in particular: Mats Arrhénborg, Björn Askerlund, Christian and Jeanette Barfod, Anna Blomberg, Kjell Blomberg, Maria Blomberg, Bengt Braun, Paul Brauns, Erik Börjesson, Thomas "Orup" Eriksson, Hans Himbert, Joakim Irebjer, Lennart Ivarsson, Anders Jelving, Harry Johans, Thomas Larsson, Christer Larsson, Johan Månsson, Joakim Norrman, Solveig och Lars Nygren, Bitte Rask, Ulf Selberg, Tom Stocklassa, Pär Wahlgren, Hasse Wetterberg, Helena Åberg, Lars Östervall.

Bergshamra and Lidingö, December 1998
Andreas af Malmborg and Ola Husberg

24′ 7″	length overall
17′ 5″	length at the waterline
5′ 11″	beam
1.8 long tons	displacement
300 sq ft	sail area

A small ship

Every boat has a story to tell but those of wooden boats are often conspicuous. The same boat may have had several owners, been modified, repaired, rebuilt, or re-rigged. That is especially true of the clipper *Sela* who has had around twenty owners since she was built over a hundred years ago. When you see her sailing over Baggensfjärden bay in Stockholm, it only feels like a short step back to the last century and the time of the Swedish painters Bruno Liljefors and Anders Zorn. The boat even resembles Zorn's boat *Mejt*. *Mejt* was twice as large as *Sela* but shared the same designer and was built at the Mälarvarv shipyard in Stockholm, 1893. *Sela's* owner Joakim Norrman has put a lot of effort into researching the boat's history. The search began in the archives of Stockholm's Maritime museum. Locating the original drawings would have been an ideal start but the effort went in vain.

The first promising leads came via another path and led back to the 1950s. A previous owner had undertaken a thorough rebuild of the boat and had documented this work with photography. These pictures revealed how *Sela's* cabin looked originally.

The Royal Library's collections were scoured along with archives of sports newspapers, old magazines, annuals, anniversary books, and sailing society material. Pictures were useful in opening up new avenues of discovery, taking the search onward. The breakthrough came when a photograph showed up in the 50th anniversary book of the Västerås sailing society. The picture showed a clipper, suspiciously similar to *Sela*, and beneath the picture appeared the name of a local pharmacist.

The Parish church in Västerås identified the pharmacist's family and, sure enough, it turned out to be the right boat. The pharmacist was no longer alive but his grandchildren who were now retired were able to help. Just by locating the name of this early owner name, the chain of ownership could be filled in both forwards and backwards through time. As the evidence was complemented with memories, log books, and pictures from family albums, the story of *Sela's* life was gradually revealed.

"She was so practical with all those cupboards in the cabin," explained one old lady over the telephone. And so it was confirmed, just as suspected, that the forecastle had previously been one huge cupboard with cupboard doors all along the inside of the planking. One old picture showed how it looked with all the details including the frames, trim, and cupboard door windows.

Sela in the midday breeze on Baggensfjärden bay outside Stockholm.

Sela has been renovated with great respect toward her original design and function.

Yet the original drawings were still missing. A second visit to the Maritime museum and another bundle of papers relating to the Mälarvarv shipyard finally yielded a clue. Amongst the papers were drawings of a one-man yacht designed by Albert Andersson, built at the Mälarvarv yard and sold for 1400 Swedish crowns ($200).

Now only the original sail plan is missing. It must be somewhere and so the search continues. *Sela's* ownership history is, nevertheless, nearly complete now with just a small gap at the end of the 19th century.

Sela came about at a time when interest in sailing was widening but sailboats were still large, commercial vessels. Small pleasure boats did not exist and few could afford a large yacht with a full crew.

This was when the idea of a smaller yacht, easier to sail and look after, and cheaper to build, came about in the KSSS (the Royal Swedish Yacht Club). The dream was of a yacht that could be sailed solo but could also accommodate two — a "one-man yacht." The only demand was that the boat be small: the length at the waterline plus the beam may not extend beyond 21 feet. The challenge was keenly set upon. Imagination flowed and draughtsmen designed everything from canoe-style cruisers and experimental cabin boats to modern fin keel boats.

One of the results of this work was *Sela*. She is in principle a "small ship," a miniature version of a 50-foot yacht. Her hull is deep, heavy, and robust, and the bow is sharp. She cuts through the water with dignity and obediently follows every murmur from the rudder. Even when there is barely any wind, she'll sniff out a breeze and move steadily

A healthy, invigorating outdoor lifestyle was the aim of Sela's former owner.

along her course. She is unusually heavy with good stability, both longitudinally and transversely, as she cautiously stamps through the waves. Tacking through narrow passes poses no problem. On a reach, she luffs up eagerly and you have to work with the tiller to keep her on course.

The hull is made from pine heartwood and the secret of her longevity is the quality of that wood. About 80 percent of the original frame, bows, and planking is still in place. She tows along a dingy from the same era, the 1890s, with a heart-shaped transom.

Although *Sela* is a one-man yacht, the designer has allowed for two to sail her. The low freeboards provide a sense of speed and

are of practical benefit when it comes to the chore of washing-up. She is a one-man boat and a one-man world, bearing many details normally found on much larger vessels. Although *Sela* is less than 25 feet long, there is a bowsprit, a chain bobstay, a self-tacking jib boom, a fife rail on the mast, and block and tackle as might be found on larger boats.

There is something very gracious and yet elegant about *Sela*. She embodies the design and seamanship of previous generations. Few boats offer their crews the chance to peak the gaff up a little or to coil the end of a line around a fife rail. Aboard *Sela*, it's important to hank on the sail in just the right way. Small details make a difference. Her owner is careful

with such matters and so equipment has turned up from various places. Some items have been redesigned and manufactured, such as the fife rail around the mast, the mainsheet car, and other rigging fittings. Food is prepared in a galley with a spirit-stove dating from the early 20th century. Crockery is stowed in bags made from sailcloth which hang inside the planking—simple, practical and functional.

Some may say that *Sela* is a cramped boat and it is true that the headroom in the cabin is not generous. But she was built for an active, outdoor lifestyle in another era where comfort takes second place. She puts you in touch with the forces of nature, sailing

The afterdeck.
The warm color tone
of the deck goes
well with the brown
mahogany and
the newly cast and
galvanized fittings.

with the water splashing against the bow, perhaps to a secluded bay for a refreshing swim before you climb onto a barren rock for your morning exercises, wearing a neatly coiffured moustache. *Sela's* task was to whisk her crew away from the shackles of town life to the bosom of nature where they could fill their lungs with fresh air, run around naked, and enjoy freedom, together with invigorating swims.

She represents a time and a sailing life where people weren't afraid of inconveniences. Indeed, small problems were part of the experience. *Sela* does not offer many home-comforts but she still manages to give a lot in return. At some level, there is a proportionality here: the more you put in, the more pleasure you get out. Equivalently, trying to create too much comfort isolates you from nature and the excitement of a challenge. *Sela* is not an entirely practical affair although it is questionable just how practical sailing is as a pursuit.

There is no engine but there is a paddle. Under the afterdeck there is an outboard motor but there is currently no way of attaching it. That will remain the case until a solution that preserves the boat's fine exterior lines can be found. If you really want a motor boat trip, it is quite possible to mount the outboard on the boat's dinghy and to have that towing alongside.

Sela carries a lot of sail for her size which makes you quite weather-dependent. Tacking is hard work and she readily takes spray onboard. You have to watch out for strong weather and be well prepared whenever you need to reef.

You need time to enjoy this style of sailing life. That feels strange in a world where time is measured everywhere and should be kept. But perhaps that is the source of relaxation and freedom: it is the feeling of being in charge of your own time, knowing that this kind of sailing takes the time it takes and is not about maximizing productivity. If you like messing around with boats—and are able to devote the necessary time—endless hours of pleasure await.

Sela's new rigging is an example of this. For her owner, it is the fruit of months of full-time work. The mast, boom and gaff are all new. Winter evenings were spent pouring over drawings for new fittings which were then cast to order, faithful to the original designs. The slightly yellow dacron sail cloth was ordered from England and resembles cotton. The sail is sewn with standing sail panels in the old-fashioned style rather than with flat panels as is the modern style. The cloth is also a little softer to handle and easier to furl.

For Joakim Norrman, who sails this one-man yacht, the work is worth every second. The payback for all those trying hours comes when you are at sea on a sunny day. Or on a July night, on a reach through the archipelago bound for the ocean as you pass the dark contours of countless islands illuminated by moonlight. All you need to enjoy it is the right instinct.

It is important that everything looks right. Things of beauty are often functional too. At sea, beauty has been a key design principle for generations. When beautiful sails are set just right, you feel a rush. The boat works with nature and the sailor can enjoy

Sela *sails outside the harbor in Västerås, August 1916.*

taking part too. To see the gaff rig pointing skyward majestically fills you with a sense of wholeness derived from cooperating with— and exploiting—the boat's personality.

Sela does not boast a dazzling finish but instead gives an impression of a well cared-for working partner. The philosophy is that as long as the boat feels fine, that's enough. An artificially high finish or brilliantly polished brass would disturb the eye.

The colors used are not striking although you can tell that *Sela's* owner has carefully studied older sailboats. He has chosen simple, original colors that chime together. Nothing stands out but together they form a charming unity. The deck is a warm cream-beige which the owner mixes himself allowing for small adjustments to be made from year to year. The freeboards are painted in a soft, warm tone. Many people choose to stain their mahogany which can result in a sharp red color. An alternative is to apply a high-quality varnish and this is what gives *Sela* her warm brown tone.

The rig plays an important role in the color balance. Stainless steel would be too grating here so the new rig fittings are galvanised instead. The gaff claw is healed with leather in the traditional manner. This gives just the right creak as the gaff kneads against the mast. The sails are not brilliant white as is the fashion on modern boats but instead they sport a yellower shade. The advantage of this is that bright light is toned down, relieving the helmsman's eyes on sunny days: yet another example of how beauty and function go hand-in-hand here.

The fife rail around the mast heel has been re-cast and galvanized, like many other fittings onboard.

Olivia I | 19
Hummingbird sloop

38' 9"	length overall
9' 2"	beam
3.5 long tons	displacement
9 knots	speed
unknown	constructor
Volvo ED6, gasoline	engine
Åbo, 1904	place of construction

Olivia II
Jugend-style sloop

40 ft	length overall
8'6"	beam
3.5 long tons	displacement
Nanni, 4 cyl diesel	engine
12 knots	speed
C Engelbrecht	constructor
Berlin, 1907	place of construction

A replica or an antique?

An antique is something old, of cultural interest. An object with whose history is, in some way, visible. It is the age and the history which give the object its interest. A replica is something quite different: a repeat, a copy of something special—perhaps of an antique. It may not always be identical to the original but there must be a close resemblance. This difference is significant in regard to the restoration of *Olivia I* and *Olivia II*, two covered pleasure boats dating from the beginning of the last century. These boats do not look like anything you see in an average harbor or boat club. They are pleasure boats unlike any other, built in the Jugend style with windowed passenger saloons. The cut-glass and leather detail in the saloons along with the panoramic windows make for a particularly inviting interior. An ornamental golden rail runs along the covering board, a detail which heightens the boat's beauty.

The first *Olivia* was built in Finland in 1904 and the second in Berlin a few years later. For years Tom Stocklassa believed he owned the most beautiful boat—*Oliva I*. Then he came across an almost identical barge owned by a Swedish priest, which had been on land since 1952. She became *Olivia II*.

This type of boat is referred to as a Hummingbird. There are many similarities with horse-drawn carriages and trams. These boats have a vertical stem, a modest sheer, low freeboards, and a rounded stern. In some ways, they resemble Stockholm's oldest Djurgård island ferries, built for transporting large groups across calm waters. But the aim here was quite different: a pleasure boat rather than a service boat. At the turn of the last century, no self-respecting aristocrat cared for a sun tan because sun tans were attributed to those who worked the land. The sight of bare skin was considered provocative. Consequently, the entire boat was covered, including the stern cockpit, to protect from the sun's rays.

Olivia II was built in Berlin, 1907. She inherited her lines from small steam barges, a style of construction which was common in Europe and the US at that time.

The hull is oak carvel-built and the superstructure is made from teak. The foredeck and afterdeck are ribbed oregon pine while the plank sheer and interior are of mahogany. From the foredeck, a staircase leads down to the saloon while the skipper has his steering place a little to port. The engine is positioned in the center of the hull under a large hood so passengers can mingle freely as they might do at a cocktail party. The glass partitions in the saloon are

exquisitely detailed and resemble the fine compartments found in railway carriages of the time. Along the sides of the saloon there are foldable seats attached to the walls. Further aft, there is a cocktail cabinet with leaded glass, a marble bench for food preparation, a small rest room, and a closet incorporating a mirror.

The German boat builders were perfectionists. The planking runs unbroken from stem to stern. The cockpit has a mahogany bench seat. The cabin sole is made of oak. Originally, a four-cylinder Daimler-Benz engine rattled away, as seen through the skylight in the engine hood. For some years now though, a modern diesel engine has been visible through this window.

As evening approaches, a thin veil of rain falls over Stockholm's Djurgårds-brunnsviken. The drizzle runs off the tightly woven roof along brass guttering. Up above, the ship's dog, Fyrtass, shakes off the raindrops.

Above: Decorative gold detailing was commonplace at the beginning of the 20th century.

Left: Olivia II's entire stern was rebuilt. The oak in her stem is naturally straight and has a dense texture.

In his own world, Tom Stocklassa restores and builds. He has an eye for beauty and applies it with sensitivity. By trade, Tom is a freelance decorative painter. He restores wall paintings and paints theater scenery. But this work is about creating a reality: one of creativity, searching, and romance. "I come from a family of artists so I have been brought up this way," he explains.

The best thing about *Olivia II*, says her owner, is that she is not built for any specific purpose. She is not for living in nor for transporting goods or people. She is simply a joy to the eye; a magnificent Prussian pleasure boat who inspires you to enjoy yourself and, at the same time, to help preserve this unique boat.

Restoring *Olivia II* was an incomparably bigger task than the work *Olivia I* required. The boat was reduced to its component parts, and the keel and all her ribs had to be replaced. The stern was disassembled and rebuilt along with new beams between the planking and decks. A priority for Tom Stocklassa was to repair rather than replace. His workshop was full of pieces of salvaged mahogany tied in bunches and labeled. Instead of replacing larger pieces, he spliced new wood into the older mahogany which was then stained and patinated, rendering the splice invisible.

Patina is a clear and visible sign of aging. The word, which is Italian and means varnish, refers to a covering which arises on objects over the course of time, due to usage and wear. In the past, patina was considered a sign of authenticity in antiques.

Preserving the boat's soul during its reconstruction was a challenge. Many

veteran boat enthusiasts have been disappointed following a rebuild. Everything looks new and fresh, yet something is missing. The boat shines as never before but something is not quite right and it is hard to say just what.

Just where is the soul of a boat to be found? Perhaps it is not in the boat's unity, not in being completely functional or shining perfectly. Is it instead in the small flaws that are proof of the boat's history? A history, a tradition, and thus a charm.

Wooden boats are often restored by taking them apart and rebuilding anew. "Newly renovated boats today resemble the interiors of banks," says Tom, which is why *Olivia II* was allowed to retain her peculiar patina. Some people might object to the pitted scars on the cabin floor caused by high-heel shoes but Tom is happy to let them be. The boat should look as though it has been lived with. Good patina arises when wood and metal have survived the sands of times, and that is something worth showing to onlookers.

"It should be complete and it should be old. Otherwise there is no difference between a replica and an antique," he says.

For Tom Stocklassa, the goal is to get on well with the boat. The enjoyment comes when the pleasure boat is used as intended. *Olivia II* should be gliding forwards across calm waters while guests eat lunch and waitresses scurry around with food and drink. In this real world of fantasy, it would not be out of place to sabre a magnum of champagne, just for the fun of it!*

Today, there is a market for chartering old wooden boats. Customers want to hire this atmosphere for an afternoon, perhaps to indulge in some photography in an unusual environment, or just to experience a journey over water in a wood-paneled Jugend-style saloon. Tom Stocklassa is at their service. When he first came across his wooden boats twenty years ago, he had no idea that things would develop like this. Now his adventure and personal pleasure have developed into something which can support him.

In the little world of *Olivia II*, there are some select antiques and meaningful decorative pieces. A small barber's kitchen for warming curling tongs was found in a florist and fitted in surprisingly well. A funnel-shaped gramophone sits on top of the engine hood and, naturally, the ship's dog is a Jack Russell, famed for appearing on "His Master's Voice" record sleeves.

As the evening approaches, paraffin lamps spread a pleasing, soft light through the saloon. There is a thought behind everything here, from the interior to the clothes. Wool is best and blue most practical for avoiding stains when you fill the paraffin lamps. Hence, Tom often wears a blue woolen blazer, also dating from the turn of the century.

For Tom Stocklass, boat life is a small platform that he is in charge of, and which he directs with his own particular finesse.

To "sabre champagne" is the tradition of opening a bottle by slicing off the neck using a sabre sword.

Olivia I *on the calm waters of her home at Djurgårdsbrunnvsiken in Stockholm.*

26	**Madam Flod**
	The Scandinavian double-ender
27′ 1″	length overall
10′ 4″	beam
approx 4 long tons	displacement
ca 480 sq ft	sail area
3′ 7″	draft
Albin 0-21	engine

A family adventure

A wooden boat can almost become a member of
the family. Over time, *Madam Flod* has grown to
be a part of the Blombergs family. Mom and Dad,
kids, relatives, pets, and acquaintances have been
carried by her generous hull. Aunts and uncles have
gotten involved with her. She is a family boat and a
lifetime project. It is as though she herself needs the
stimulation and interest of the people around her.
The project had a beginning, and perhaps there's an
end somewhere, but it is the present that counts.
Madam represents comfort and tradition while the
world all around is ever-changing. It doesn't matter
that she moves slowly through the water, or that a
handle is awkward to use, or that maintenance is so
time-consuming. There is time and there are willing
hands. She sits in the water as stable as iron, tied up
at her home mooring.

Kjell Blomberg is *Madam's* owner but he knows neither where or by whom she was built. There is some information to suggest that she was once the flagship for the Katarina Sea Scout troop in Stockholm where she sailed with fourteen young boys aboard. Kjell first met her 30 years ago and immediately fell for her—a strong, gaff-rigged Scandinavian double-ender made from heavy oak, fairly standard were it not for one eye-catching oddity: both the stem and sternpost are bowed in a curious manner. This is known as "home-longing" in some circles, referring to the way the lines bend back toward the hull.

For Kjell, who is an architect, *Madam* represents the boat of all boats. She has a past when she went by the name of *Rustica* which suits her character: traditional, strong, broad, and a little stocky.

Inboard, a clear sense of history prevails: the atmosphere inside the cabin causes many to pause and draw breath. The water lapping against the clenched oak tells of times past and sea adventures. The frame is made from pine and the joints are secured with wooden pins called trunnels. The panels in the cabin roof and the beaded wood paneling in the forward bulkhead each have their own stories to tell. The solid natural wooden sides of the cockpit, the hard iron of the traveler on the afterdeck, and the cast iron chain plate... each detail is a tunnel through time. The music of the water blends reality with myth to create an experience which invites you to indulge your own fantasy. The sunlight playing off

The details on the rig:
simple, functional—and ancient.

of the varnish, the smell of linseed oil and tar, aged paintwork, and the creaking of the rigging sharpen the feeling further. Reflecting light and shifting shades of red and green provide the backdrop.

At some point in *Madam Flod's* past, the cabin has been rebuilt: there are clear signs of a previous entrance from the deck on port side. Previously, there were tightly placed bulkheads towards the forward cabin and

between the saloon and cockpit by the stern. Perhaps this was for safety reasons: water would have been trapped in the cockpit without getting in to the cabin. Maybe there was a storage or freight area here. There are signs to indicate that the cockpit had been roofed over at one stage. *Madam* invites you to imagine the scene.

The unusual, round steering well to the stern where the helmsman sits, separated

from the rest of the crew, is an historic curiosity. *Madam* also has a long bowsprit to bear the headsail. Most of the rigging is made from wood and iron—not corrosion-free because that would be wrong, says Kjell. Cleats and pulleys were turned from wood in the old-fashioned manner. Kjell is, however, careful not to get hung up on kitschy details. There are no extravagances onboard, just simple, functional solutions.

Madam is continually being modified and renovated, "not with piety but quite high-handedly," as Kjell puts it. He simply began where there was most necessity and involved other areas as needed. While sailing in heavy seas north of Åland, the boat's tarred oakum started pushing in to the boat after some iron rivets had rusted away and boards began bending. A lot of putty was needed to make her tight.

It all began during winter 1976-77. Since then, Kjell has spent most of his spare time during the winter half of the year working with *Madam Flod* and has had help from friends and relatives. He dares not guess how much time has been put in: in principle, it is every weekend. Piece by piece the hull was taken apart, moulds taken, and new parts produced and remounted. At different times, *Madam* has been missing her boarding, underside, bows, keel, and deck.

Something which started small without great ambition gradually grew into a total rebuild. The plan was not to take on the whole boat but the turning point came when Kjell had to replace the keel and bows. Then he realized he could manage the whole boat so *Madam Flod* became almost new again.

Since then, he has learnt to fell oaks with a 4 foot diameter, saw them, and plank them in to suitably-sized pieces. Oak has traditionally been considered the best timber. It is the heaviest and most compact of all the usual woods used in boat bulding. Its heartwood is pale brown and resinous but the sapwood is inferior: it becomes pale, dry, and porous over time. The best timber has annual rings which are about $\frac{1}{5}$ to $\frac{1}{3}$ inch in width.

If the timber is good, the newly felled oak will smell fresh and slightly acidic. Another indicator of the wood's quality is found by knocking a plank: a high-pitched, open sound is a good sign. If the sound is hollow or deep, the wood may be of a lesser grade. A dull sound might mean that rot is setting in. Generally, though, oak withstands rot well because of its natural resins. Oak is hard, durable, and can be used both in planking and for load-bearing applications such as in the frame or floor timbers, although it does shrink and swell considerably.

Boat-building timber should be thoroughly dried to avoid the risk of shrinkage occurring after construction is complete, which could cause leakage. Kjell used new oak in the hull which had been subjected to a drying method he developed himself. The freshly sawn oak was wrapped in plastic and warmed up by sunlight or a strong halogen lamp. This causes the wood to sweat; moisture forms inside the plastic and then runs off. The planks do not crack because the surface of the wood remains wet and the surrounding air is moist.

In a boat with a rounded stem and stern such as *Madam Flod*, there are many curved and bent wooden pieces. For these, Kjell uses naturally-grown timber. He has figured out his own way of steaming the planks: he rubs linseed oil into them and then heats the upper side with a blow-torch until the underside feels warm. This drives the damp out of the wood, allowing it to be bent and joined into place.

He has taught himself everything he needed to know during the course of this 31 year project, yet still feels unable to call himself a wooden boat builder. When setting

Old blocks are kept and restored. They still work perfectly well.

The light filters through into Madam Flod's cabin.

out on a new task, he often feels he is "all fingers and thumbs, but you just have to give it time…" says Kjell.

The floor timbers have not needed any work but the planking has been replaced. The internal ballast is now provided by a solid steel beam running under the keel. A lead-filled pipe provides a further half ton of ballast. Nevertheless, *Madam* is still quite yielding and so you have to take care when setting the sails, reefing and swapping often. The sail wardrobe is generous so the sail area can be tuned by changing jibs or by tucking a reef in the main or foresail. On a boat rigged with a gaffer, topsail, jib, and second staysail, this keeps you busy.

For Kjell Blomberg, the attraction lies in facing new problems: to reflect upon them and then solve them. Manufacturing his own tools, developing his own methods, putting them in to practice and confirming theory with reality is all part of the allure.

Living with *Madam* demands skill, knowledge, and imagination. Sometimes the task feels too great in its consumption of time, money, and work. Yet the problems can never be larger than the boat and so are surmountable, if tackled systematically, piece-by-piece. Making progress may be painstaking, requiring hard work and money, but, at the end of the day, the limits are set only by one's own capabilities.

Madam is a typical family boat. Kjell's daughter Maria grew up onboard. "Just being able to sleep here is special," she says. For her, *Madam Flod* represents being with the family, along with a little nostalgia.

Madam Flod is a secure pleasure boat: speed is not important. She picks up well on

a beam reach and a quarter-wind but crosses poorly and is slowed up by a headwind.

Onboard, a camp-style life awaits you, with tinned food, fresh water, and a camping stove, which all work very well, as long as you have patience. She does not sail readily on open seas, demanding as she does respect for the winds and the weather. Nevertheless, Sweden's east coast is rich in archipelagoes and other sheltered sailing spots where she spends many weeks each year, always receiving a warm welcome on these cruises.

When the Blomberg family, father and daughter, sail out, they take supplies of juice, coffee, and biscuits with them. The daughter looks up and wonders, "Have you read *Exterminate All the Brutes* by Sven Lindqvist? It paints a fascinating picture about how racism can arise…"

He mutters something sympathetic in reply. She sits back at the tiller while he scrambles about on the foredeck, hooks up sails and adjusts tackle. The jib and staysail are set windward, the gaff is hoisted with just the right peak. After much effort, a few extra turns and an uncooperative topping lift, the topsail is eventually hoisted. The process looks cumbersome and takes time, but there is time to spend. Kjell willingly spends time doing this more than anything else. It is a warm August afternoon but most people have given up hope of a good summer and returned to town. Maybe that's why the bay of Nämndöfjärden looks like a newly-laid floor. There is a slight breeze as *Madam Flod* disappears into the blueness without the slightest hint of homesickness, into the excitement of a family adventure.

Above: The foredeck is a web of blocks, sheets, and fittings for the headsail.

Right: Strawberry squash in the food box, the kettle, and petroleum-oil stove in the galley.

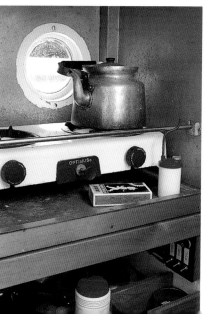

Kerma
Skerry Cruiser 95

61' 6"	length overall
9' 4"	beam
10.3 long tons	displacement
1020 sq ft	sail area
7' 10"	draft
Stockholm's Motorboat yard, 1918	place of construction

Guppy
Skerry Cruiser 15

21' 4"	length overall
14' 5"	length at the waterline
5' 1"	beam
1300 lbs	displacement
160 sq ft	sail area
3 ft	draft

Still the quickest

The 95-footer moves swiftly across the lake. The water appears dead calm and yet somehow she pushes on. It just takes a few brisk cats' paws and off she shoots; her size and weight help her maintain speed. *Kerma* is as fast as a modern 40-footer and lives up to her handicap rating of 1.30. There is something special about a skerry cruiser; she carries her lines with a lofty confidence. Skerry cruisers are still some of the fastest boats around despite their 90 years. As the undisputed queens of these waters, their superiority carries with it perhaps a hint of arrogance. In the golden past of the skerry cruisers, every yacht has a unique essence with its own history, racing merits, famed owners and builders.

Skerry cruisers come in nine classes with sail areas of 15, 22, 30, 40, 55, 75, 95, 120, and 150 square meters (from around 230 to 1600 square feet). Most of the boats are of the 22 and 30 classes but the larger classes are also well represented. No two skerry cruisers are quite alike; each has its own design and unique blend of length, beam, displacement, and sail area. If a designer opts for a long, fast waterline, the displacement, keel length, beam, or the height of the freeboards must be increased. The rules defining the skerry cruiser class specify in detail the minimum dimensions of the frame, planking, and decks. Everything down to the size of the smallest screw and how it should be fitted is described in tables and pictures.

The original rules were drawn up in 1908 but have been revised a few times. The first skerry cruisers were sailboats with standard proportions but they became longer and more extreme over time. The rule changes were meant to ensure the boats would not become staid but the rule makers did not always keep up with the latest developments. The temptation to create the fastest yacht could become too great. The most extreme examples were built in the early 1920s when a skerry cruiser could be long, fragile, and as a narrow as a canoe. They were sailed hard and competed intensively yet it was not unheard of for a boat to collapse when brought on land. Without the upward forces from the mast and stays, the boat could suffer a reverse sheer in the deck line, known as a "cat's back."

In the world of the skerry cruiser, beauty is both a goal in itself and an important pre-requisite for positive racing

characteristics. "Beautiful boats sail well" was a respected design principle long before the time of large-hulled dinghies and lateral underwater bodies. Beauty brings with it speed which is another distinctive attribute of skerry cruisers. Racing close to the water in a yacht with low freeboards is enticing.

Kerma heels readily, lying stoutly on her side with the leeward gunwale lapping at the water surface. The speed-inducing water-line increases when she heels. She obeys every murmur from the rudder. In changing tack, the hull rotates crisply, almost exactly around her mid-point. She is a sailboat built without compromise. The combination of beauty, speed, and maneuverability is unbeatable. Only a designer of a skerry could dream up a boat with 320 square foot of sail which is only 42 foot long with a 6 foot beam. Or one with dimensions of 62 foot by 9, carrying over 1000 square foot of sail, as *Kerma* does. The skerry cruiser is, quite simply, a yacht. "Slender and swift. That is what sums up yacht, is it not?" contemplates her owner, Hasse Wetterberg.

The special experience comes from the low freeboards and proximity to water. But *Kerma* should not heel too far; she often sails better if you take in a reef. About 20 degrees of heel suits her well, sailing more comfortably and sometimes more quickly.

Kerma was built in 1918 at Stockholm's motorboat yard, with an oregon pine deck and mahogany interior. In her original form, she was rigged with a gaff, in keeping with many other yachts of the time. The boat was

Kerma means "cream" in Finnish. She belongs to the cream of skerry cruisers.

ordered by Georg Wrang of Stockholm but was soon sold to the Gothenburg shipowner, Arnold Wilson. He named her *Kerma* which is the Finnish word for cream.

Kerma was designed and built for racing. In the 1920s she often beat her larger sisters, the 120 and 150 class skerry cruisers. She has been rebuilt and modified several times to help maintain her advantage. In the mid-1970s, she underwent a particularly thorough renovation when she received a new lead keel, new deadwood, a new underwater hull and a stainless steel rudder. A steel mast foot was cast and fitted, being significantly stronger than the previous construction. The bows were replaced and a new inner stem was fitted to further strengthen the hull. This was a 23 foot internally-mounted oak beam which runs forward from a point behind the mast. Over the years, the stern had begun to sag slightly. This was lifted, and the hull seams were resealed, so correcting the sheer which now follows exactly the same line as it did when she was first built, as demonstrated by some early photographs. The deck layout was revised with *Kerma* receiving a purpose-built cockpit. A 27 horsepower engine was installed in 1988, *Kerma's* 70th year.

In a near-gale one November on the Nämndöfjärden, *Kerma* broke her wooden mast that she had borne since 1939. She now has a custom-built glass fibre mast which is strong and adjustable. The mainsail now has full-length battens which, after a few teething problems, work well. Although she is missing much of the equipment now expected on a modern racing yacht, and is not sailed by a professional racing crew, she

Above: Skerry cruisers in a race on Gripsholmsviken.

Right: Thanks to her broad stern, SK 15 Guppy sails fast in leading wind.

Opposite: Kerma's cockpit has been rebuilt to modern racing standards.

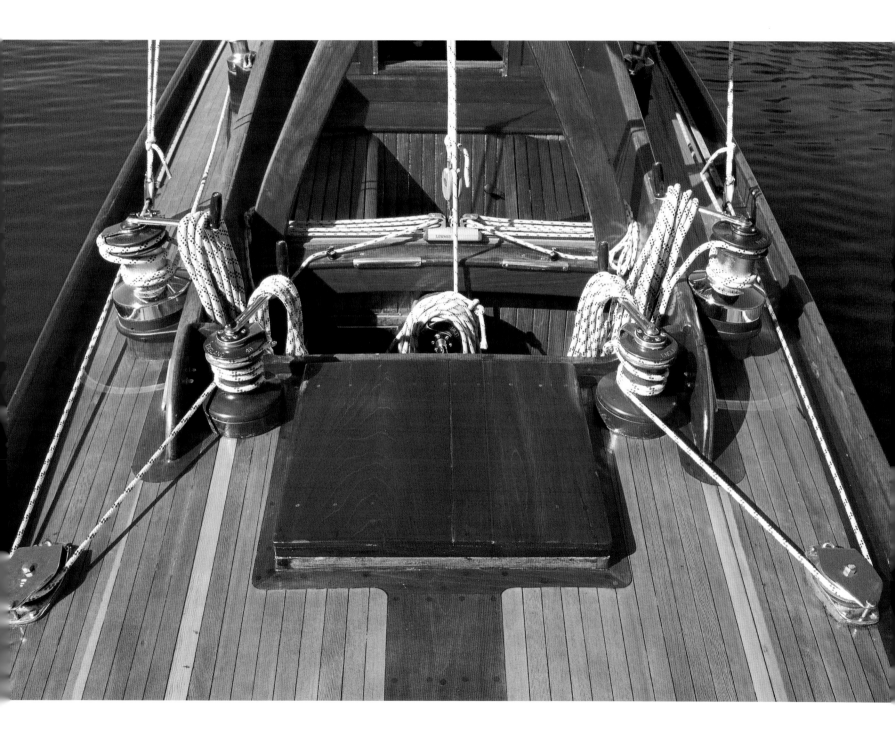

still keeps up with the competition. "We think it's fun and we do well enough," says her owner. She also spends time on long-distance and day-sailing trips, covering at least 2000 nautical miles in a season. She has seen Sweden's west and south coasts and crossed the Baltic sea to Finland.

Kerma is not alone: most of the big, old skerry cruisers live on. Only a handful have disappeared, caught fire, or fallen into disrepair. They are so unique, and cost so much to maintain, that they are usually well-cared for by their owners. The naval architect who designed her in 1910, Erik Salander, was successful on the racing circuit and was also responsible for several noted 40 and 50 class skerry cruisers, in addition to one of the smallest, a 15 class.

Paul Brauns came across a skerry cruiser on land at the Öregrund sailing club. The boat was for sale but no one knew much about it. Paul began investigating and ended up at the archives of the Maritime History Museum in Stockholm. There he found drawings of a 160 square foot skerry cruiser and all the measurements agreed. The plans were dated 1916 and signed by Erik Salander, who had designed *Kerma* a few years later. *Guppy's* identity was established.

When Paul found *Guppy*, her bottom was holed. A previous owner had added lead to the keel and replaced the original rig with a marconi rig, which is a complicated modern rig with sheer on the masthead towards the stern. The stays and shrouds had been driven in so hard that several floor timbers had cracked and the planking was damaged.

With the help of designer Erik Söderblom, Paul Brauns rebuilt her to match the original

appearance as closely as possible. *Guppy* had a new garboard strake, three floor timbers were replaced, and new decking and a small shelter cabin were installed. A new mast and boom were built and she now sails with her original gaff rig once again, restored to Eric Salander's vision.

Wherever she goes, *Guppy* is usually the smallest boat in the crowd with a length at the waterline of just over 13 feet. She is a classic day sailboat with a small keel and low sail plan. She is stiff, sharing attributes from both smaller dinghies and considerably larger boats. She is fast on a beam reach and on a run. The long stern is buoyant and leaves a trail of bubbles in her wake.

Paul is also building a new 22 class skerry cruiser for himself. He dreams of building Salander-designed boats on a larger scale and exporting them. There is a lot of interest in these Swedish veteran designs abroad. Perhaps a skerry cruiser 15 could be sold in Germany, Norway, or even Japan. A traditionally-built skerry cruiser, with carvel planking made from quarter-sawn pine heartwood from northern Sweden, floor timbers, bows, and frame of oak, saturated with linseed oil... coaming, interior, toe rails, cabin, and tiller in mahogany... a cabin roof of beaded spruce panels. All spars in clear Swedish, tightly-ringed spruce, with six coats of varnish... does that not sound appealing?

The skerry cruiser is a unique, very Swedish type of boat. For many, it embodies the very idea of how a yacht should look: long, sleek, low freeboards, and a tall mast with a little sheer at the top. This is a boat built without compromise: a thing of beauty designed to maximize the sailing experience.

48' 2"	*length overall*
8' 4"	*beam*
6 long tons	*displacement*
12 knots	*cruising speed*
Ford diesel, 80 hp	*engine*
C.G. Pettersson	*constructor*
Kristinehamn, 1913	*place of construction*

"Of the return journey, nothing can be said except that it was spent in the company of coffee, liqueurs, and cigars as we praised the successful trip, the comfortable boat, and the exceptionally reliable engine which, on that first test-drive, worked hard for almost ten hours without a hint of complaint."
signed V.G., Swedish Motor Magazine, 1911

Inside Pettersson's saloon

Feeling pleasantly satisfied after lunch at Furusund's inn, consisting of smorgasbord, cauliflower purée, fillet of pike, caper sauce, roast beef, and portuguese onions washed down with a couple of bottles of well-chilled Burgundy, we embarked upon the return journey to the capital. That was the scene on April 2, 1911, the maiden voyage of *Viking III*, owned by C.G. Pettersson. Five high-spirited gentlemen, "and one so-called guest," had set off from Slussen in central Stockholm and made their way north through the ice-floe for Furusund. For these men, life onboard was an everyday adventure, a refreshing outdoor excursion in jolly company along with good food and drink.

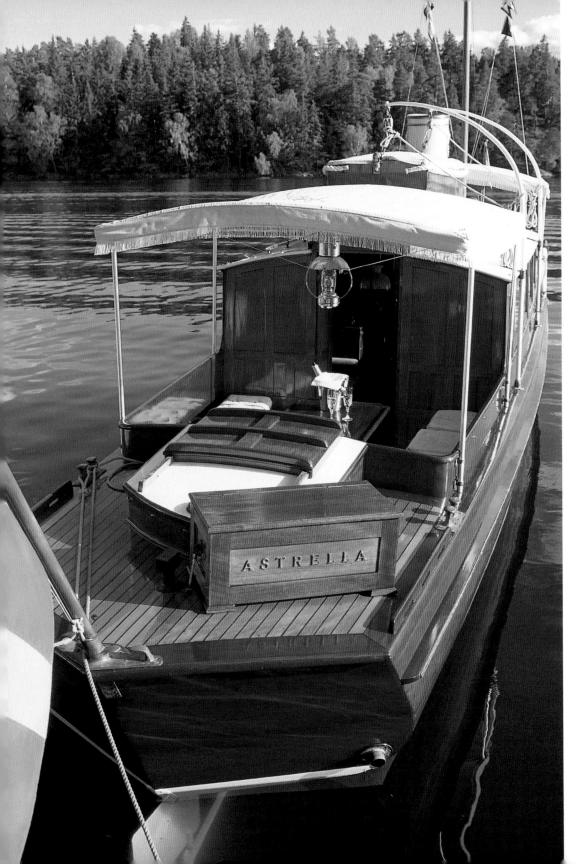

C.G. Pettersson, often pictured with a cigar and skipper's cap, is probably Sweden's most well-known designer of pleasure boats. He gave his name to a particular type of boat. The Pettersson boat is a carvel-built motor boat with a straight stem, a long, narrow hull, small keel, an open cockpit, and a fairly tight cabin under the foredeck. A distinctive feature is the ears: the curved line of the gunwale between the raised foredeck and the lower covering board allows for a raised cabin roof and more space down below.

Pettersson designed his boats to be slender so they could move through the water with ease. Engines of the day were not powerful and so speeds were only moderate at best. A 26 foot boat could reach only 7 knots with a 6 horsepower engine, covering 12 nautical miles per gallon of gas. Pettersson boats were generally frugal in their gas consumption.

C.G. Pettersson was the son of a farmer from Ramsö, a village on Sweden's east coast. He studied engineering and designed tugs, working boats, and fishing boats. His fame, though, arose from his pleasure boats.

"CGP," as he was known, designed boats for the cream of Swedish society and other famous people. For the artist Bruno Liljefors, he designed a canoe and a motor cruiser. Pettersson often visited Liljefors at his studio in Stockholm's archipelago.

During the first half of the twentieth century, boat building was a complicated procedure requiring close cooperation between the customer, designer, and builder. First the customer would go to an architect to explain how his dream boat should look. The architect would make drawings, discuss them with the customer, and revise them accordingly. When the customer was satisfied, cost estimates were requested from a number of shipyards.

The building instructions were clear and precise. For one motor cruiser, CGP specified that the stem should be of dried oak, free of cracks, the coaming should be of Honduran mahogany, the oars of ash dressed in leather with copper banding. All timber should be of first-class quality, with even coloring, and it should not be gnarled or knotted. CGP personally ensured the work was carried out precisely according to instructions, occasionally demanding that the boat builder replace areas of planking, a covering board or a piece of edging trim.

CGP further instructed that the after-cabin should be furnished with "the sole in teak and there should be storage in African mahogany for 10 liters of liqueur, 25 bottles of mineral water, and 25 bottles of pilsner."

The *Astrella* is a genuine saloon-boat with a veranda mounted on a narrow hull. Circular portlights stretch along the freeboards toward the steep stem. Magnificent brass stanchions along the foredeck tell of her origins. *Astrella* is a yacht with grand dimensions. The stem is proud and the texture of the wood impressive.

The boat houses eight berths in two cabins located for and aft of the spacious amidship saloon. The crew's simple bunks are found in the forward cabin; the rest of that cabin is used for storing lines and wet-weather clothing. In the forward cabin, there are two bunks along the sides with closets.

Astrella's *large vents help to air the forward cabin beneath the generous foredeck.*

The steering position is exposed although there is a woven roof mounted on bowed rails. The foot board here is raised and conceals the Ford diesel engine beneath. The steering position is simply equipped with modernized controls. Aft of the steering position, down a staircase, lies the magnificent marine toilet, made of brass. The pantry is located on the opposite side.

Inside the large saloon, you sit comfortably in the plushness of the green sofas and coordinated light green drapes. On the foot boards lie thick carpets and a wood stove crackles in the corner. Towards the aft cockpit sit two sets of drawers, crowned with ornate guard rails; a silky matte finish gives the mahogany a beautiful luster. The fore-saloon is furnished in the same resplendent colors.

The aft cockpit has plenty of space for socializing and relaxing beneath the canopy. The wholesaler Georg Tempelman entertained guests here, as did other important figures of Swedish society such as the shipowner Gustav Erikson and the journalist Kar de Mumma. Pleasure and well-being are just as important to the current owners, Lars and Gunilla Östervall. *Astrella* is a summer home: the family uses her every weekend of the season, stretching into November.

Astrella is a large boat, yet there is not enough headroom to stand up straight in the aft cabin. The anchor and anchor line are stowed in a mahogany chest on the aft deck. A large flag at the stern completes the picture. The boat is equipped with heating, running hot and cold water, a refrigerator with ice compartment, a stove, and an oven.

Above: Boat builder Thomas Larsson loosens one of Astrella's *old keel timbers, dating from 1913.*

Left: New keel timbers and a stem are put in to position. New rib ends are fitted here too.

With four large glass windows along each side, she resembles a horse-drawn carriage. Beauty is important; her owner could not contemplate sailing a boat which was not beautiful. Her lines make her special, together with the fact that despite her 85 years of age, she is still varnished perfectly. The owners of many of her contemporaries have given up trying to rid the hull of nicks and faults, choosing to simply paint her white.

Astrella's owner has gone in the other direction. Do not make unnecessary changes; restore in preference to replace. Authenticity and patina are preserved which makes her unique and exclusive. The brasswork is not highly polished, with the exception of the magnificent toilet. It is as though the boat's essence would be disturbed if you rubbed to hard.

In common with most other wooden boats of her time, *Astrella* has undergone extensive restoration. 180 feet of planking, the transom, and the foredeck with bulkheads all had to be replaced. Learning about marine carpentry, cover making, or engine maintenance can be an exciting challenge which many wooden boat owners proudly take on themselves. Yet there are many talented professionals who can also be called upon.

As a manager in the construction industry, Lars Östervall has learned how to "divide and conquer": breaking up large projects into smaller ones and finishing each task before beginning the next. Lars has done much of the restoration work himself, but not all of it. After 16 years he has nearly covered the whole boat, although "finished" is not an expression which wooden boat owners

This lifeboat has been
around for a large part of
Astrella's life. The chimney
with its "KMK" emblem
(representing the Royal
Swedish Motorboat Club) is
a more modern addition.

tend to use. When the keel timbers, stem, garboard strake, and some bow planking needed to be replaced, the highly experienced assistance of Thomas Larsson and Harry Johans was enlisted.

The work begins with obtaining the necessary timber. The oak is still a 20 foot long tree when Harry Johans begins sawing. It is then worked on by hand with a chisel, plane, rule, bevel, and other tools.

The garboards, stem, and keel are inspected. Rotten wood is replaced. The keel timbers from 1913 are then dismantled. The rabbet is formed using a rebate plane on the new keel timbers. This is where the planking will join to the keel. The stem and keel timbers are put into position and joined with strong deadwood. New rib ends and some floor members are manufactured in stainless steel and then fitted. Old meets new as replacement mahogany is joined with mahogany that is over 85 years old.

The moisture level in the timber is measured and found to be around 8-10 percent. The value for the old hull was 17-18 percent. To fit the planking, template planks are used with true points which match up with each rib. Yet much still rests upon instinct, how it looks, and experience. You need an eye for this kind of work. The planks are twisted and turned in many ways.

Poisonous red –lead oxide is still the best way of protecting the wood from rot but it may only be applied by trained professionals with appropriate protection under controlled conditions. The old ways are still the best for many aspects of this craft. The mixture of linseed oil, lead oxide, and mutton tallow used for treating the keel rabbit is

unchanged. Tallow seals the joints between planks as it has done for generations. The compound gives a little with the wood and never dries out.

A soft layer of pink dust covers the boat and the smell of shavings reaches your nose inside this huge plastic hangar. A solid brass bow fitting is being milled and ground. It will then be grooved, soldered, and welded to the stem. The end result is very elegant.

"It must be beautiful for you to be satisfied," says Harry. Ensuring the restoration is of the same class as the original is the calling of boat restorers. Yet too much perfection can also be a problem. With today's modern tools, adhesives and techniques, the finish can be too perfect. Time should be allowed to leave its mark.

Astrella is a floating summer house. She is used by the family throughout the summer and long into fall.

27' 10"	length excluding bowsprit
36' 1"	length overall
10' 10"	beam
540 sq ft	sail area
5 ft	draft
52 ft	mast height
Yanmar YSE 12, diesel	engine
Lysekil, 1897	place of construction

The art of determination

She stands upright in the corner of a shipyard on the coast outside of Stockholm. All her dignity is there to behold, a dignity that comes from unifying tradition with functionalism and an aesthetic beauty. It is all about her permanent and unyielding form. *Lovisa's* attraction lies not in some superficial, cosmetic beauty but instead in the play between something with both an inner beauty and a purpose. Aware as she is of her tradition, she carries herself with pride, almost to the point of arrogance. The scratches, nicks, cracks, and dents create a living surface which is accentuated by a glossy veil of varnish. She is as as strong as a powerful ship and yet as slender as a rowing boat. As dignified as an old lady, she yearns like a teenager.

Lovisa is partly a working boat and partly a racing boat. On a beam or broad reach, she sails past many more modern boats.

How else could her covering boards have been created? Take an oak plank, 8" by 1," plane it to just the right shape and steam it soft so it can be bent from the stem to sternpost. Then result is one long, living, stretched, well-balanced line which sustains itself and basks in its own clearly-defined unequivocalness. Dizzily low in the center, it rises high in defiance at the stem.

How could that upturned nose be any different? If you are going to meet the high seas with a stem, it had better be like this. *Lovisa* invites you to touch her, to take hold of the powerful mooring bollards ahead of the forecastle hatch, to stroke her aging planking, or to carefully set foot on the oregon pine ribbed deck.

Is she a holiday boat dating from the turn of the last century? A fishing boat or a pilot boat? No one can say for sure although there is no doubt that she has her roots in the west coast of Sweden. The lines, her heritage, and that sheer point to the town of Lysekil. The sheer rises ahead of the forecastle hatch towards the stem. The two foot wide deck stretches the full length of the boat. It lies temptingly close to the water and frames the world that is *Lovisa*. Like many other similar boats from the area, she is narrower at the stern than the bow. This makes the hull heavy and stable, and also makes her powerful and fast.

Lovisa was built in 1897 with oak planking, heavy ribs of heartwood pine, and a keel of red-beech. She was originally rigged with a gaff but has now inherited a mast from an R6

class boat and also boasts a self-tacker and a roller genoa. She is a Scandinavian double-ender and was registered as number 13 in the "Fram" sailing club.

The "Fram" sailing club was formed in Gothenburg in 1896 and was aimed at the working class. The idea was that craftsmen and workers in industry should also be able to enjoy sailing, not just merchants and directors. The "Frams" were young men from the yards and workshops who did not feel at home in the finer sailing societies, but still longed for the seas and sailing.

There were two ways of obtaining a boat. Often, a tired old fishing boat was bought for a few crowns, then decked and rigged, a cabin built, and furnished. The alternative was to get hold of some timber and build one yourself. Whichever approach was chosen, several members always worked together on the project.

At the turn of the century, the fishermen of the west coast began renewing and motorizing their fleet, which meant a lot of their sailboats went on to the market and could be picked up cheaply. These were trawlers, mackerel fishing boats, or pilot boats built in the mid 1800s which had been sailed hard over many years before, and in some cases, abandoned along the coastline. The Frams gave them new homes, rigged them, and spruced them up. In doing so, the club members saved a cultural inheritance and also created a modern racing boat. They created tables of holding power and decided upon rules for the dimensions of their boats. Thanks to their solid construction, these boats built a reputation for durability, even over long periods of rough conditions.

Almost every year, the club ordered a new boat from one of the yards or they bought an old hull, refitted it, and rigged it.

It was common at that time to sail with two spritsails, a topsail, a jib, and another staysail. The sprit rig was common on fishing boats while yachts and pleasure boats usually had a gaff rig with a top sail, jib, and additional staysail. In the 1910s, the Frams began measuring sail area in order to divide their boats into classes. This led to the demise of the topsail and additional staysail which often caused difficulties when racing.

A genuine Fram double-ender is clinker-built in oak, with strong, sloping sides and a sharp, slender bottom. The planking is varnished and the deck is seamed. For a long time, it was blasphemy to fit an engine to your boat. Doing so led to expulsion from the sailing club. A Fram double-ender was for sailing and if there was no wind, you could always scull along with oars.

That attitude is now a little softer: *Lovisa* has an engine and no one complains about it. Her owner's name is Hans Himbert and he bought her in 1976 and sailed for three seasons. Then she began leaking too much and so he brought her up on land.

That is where she stayed for 19 years. Over that time, Hans has replaced the stem, ribs, and floor timbers. He has lowered the keel and replaced some 280 feet of the one-inch oak planking. Fifteen years ago, he was fortunate enough to come across a consignment of boat timber from the Neglinge yard at Saltsjöbaden. The planks were wide, 50 year old, carefully selected heartwood which is something of a treasure today because it is hard to obtain slow-grown timber of high quality.

Hans is a designer and so is used to grappling with the aesthetic balance between form and function. At work, there are many interests and opinions to be consolidated but with *Lovisa*, Hans Himbert does as he pleases, without compromise. There is no need to ask or gain permission because this is his time, his patience, his money, and his work.

Hans is not in a hurry; he does not have to finish soon. "I have learnt to be satisfied before actually finishing," he says placidly. The dream is for the boat to be strong, healthy, and well planned, throughout. Anything that is in poor condition, rotten, or not working needs to be replaced so that *Lovisa* may live for another hundred years. It needs to be well built and to look good but it must not be—or appear to be—brand new.

The details must be beautiful, thorough, and appropriate. The inboard space needs to be well planned so that *Lovisa* is a pleasant boat to sail and live with. Not everything has to be as it was originally; *Lovisa* was gaff rigged previously and may never have had a cabin but just an open space for transporting people and goods. To restore her along those lines might be correct historically but Hans chooses what feels right, what adds beauty, and what suits the boat. With this mindset, modern solutions may be justifiable. For example, *Lovisa* now has a ⅞ rig from a 20 foot R-class yacht rather than the old gaff rig. The mast is now 7 feet longer too. Just as the Frams intended, Hans likes a lot of

To reinforce the impression of form and volume, Lovisa has no bulkheads. Shiny new ribs contrast with the older, darkening ones.

The starting line-up for the Fram club's big anniversary regatta in 1906 at Rivö in Gothenburg's southern archipelago.

"All boys dream of a wooden boat, bronze in color from tarring, shiny from varnish and salt spray. Her nose was high, and confidently she cut through the water with her sail full."

Knut Larsson, "Halkip"

sail. *Lovisa* can take it but if the wind does freshen, you can always reef. Who decides what is right and what feels good? That's Hans Himbert.

She has had new glued ribs to replace the old ones. A challenging problem was how to provide standing room in the cabin without raising the roof which would have spoiled the craft's natural lines. The solution was to replace the floor timbers with stainless steel members. These are not as tall and so the cabin sole can be fitted lower down which solves the problem. Raising the cabin roof was not an option. "That would have destroyed the whole boat," says Hans, quite sincerely. Widening the cabin was not possible either because that would have diluted the character of this genuine Fram double-ender.

Hans fits in with his boat; he is improving its function and its strength but he also has his own demands. For example, there are no bulkheads on the boat, "to create a

sense of volume and to expose the boat's construction." There is nothing wrong with some parts looking a little darker or older than others as long as there is no rotting, of course. In the dim light down below, shapes and colors blend together, new ribs stand beside older ones and fresh trunnels mingle with others that are over a hundred years old.

Previously, Hans was keen on finishing the project as soon as possible, to re-launch her and start sailing. That is no longer the case—the family will have to wait a little longer. He is not concerned that the boat will never be finished, even if others are starting to wonder, after 18 years of work. "Is the boat in the water yet?" they tease him.

In fact, *Lovisa* was in the sea for the summer of 1997 when she had her hundredth birthday. Hans does not care if people think he is just a little bit mad. "*Lovisa* is not a wreck which will never be ready. She is a hobby."

It is not a chore to go down to the boat two evenings a week. He is still enthusiastic although there are times when he takes a break. It is quite possible to take a holiday in Greece with the family, or to sail other boats even though *Lovisa* is not finished. He has stopped trying to put a time limit on when she will be ready and in the water.

There have been years when no progress has been made on *Lovisa*. Children, houses, businesses, and family all have their demands on his time too, meanwhile yard rental and material costs keep on growing. But the work on *Lovisa* continues, if not rapidly then certainly with determination.

Match II
Motor yacht

46 ft	length overall
8' 6"	beam
5 long tons	displacement
14 knots	speed
Ford diesel, 6-cyl, 115 hp	engine
Knut Ljungberg	constructor
Lidingö, 1918	place of construction

Loris
Express cruiser

49 ft	length overall
7' 10"	beam
5.9 long tons	displacement
30 knots	speed
Cummins diesel, 300 hp	engine
Knut Ljungberg	constructor
Hästholmsvarvet Stockholm, 1913	place of construction

Kreuger's babes

Successful businessmen and industry leaders have been hugely important for wooden pleasure boats. At the turn of the last century, it was fashionable to own an elegant sail or motor yacht. To own several was an even greater status symbol; some directors ordered a new boat each year. The rush of orders created plenty of work for constructors such as C.G. Pettersson, Knut Ljungberg, Henning Forslund, Jac M. Iverson, and Ruben Östlund. The shipyards had a busy time. A beautiful motor yacht was an unmistakable sign of affluence and status. With the sea breeze rushing past their ears, top directors could relax wearing a sailor's uniform and a skipper's cap bearing the KSSS emblem of the Royal Swedish Sailing Society. It was not just the outdoor life but also the social aspects that were attractive. The speed of these craft injected yet more excitement.

The king of the matchstick industry, Ivar Kreuger, owned Sweden's fastest boats, which were often seen sweeping past, between the office in Stockholm and the summerhouse in Kansholmsfjärden. Kreuger's boats were used for entertaining. When Ivar Kreuger shot himself in Paris, his matchstick empire collapsed and his boats were sold at auction in Jansson's shipyard, Fittja, in June 1932.

The motor yacht *Match II* was one of the boats up for sale. *Match II* was ordered in 1917, designed by the engineer Knut Ljungberg and built at the Gustafsson & Andersson yard at Lidingö. Like other Ljungberg boats, it was long, slender and stunning. Ljungberg was famous for his artistic pen; no other designer drew boats with such a gentle sheer and long, flowing lines. Also typical were the long bows, a large engine room, a low midships saloon, unbroken exterior line and an extended stern. It was a little impractical and not the most efficient use of space but fantastic to look at. These were fast boats too; length lends itself to speed. Ljungberg's creations were known for the way they furrowed the waves, with water sweeping over the decks.

For Krister Littorn, Kreuger's closest colleague and a director in the matchstick empire, Knut Ljungberg designed a 46 foot motor yacht in Honduran mahogany with stretched bows, an open steering position, and a spacious saloon. Littorin helped design the interior and made sure the yacht could comfortably sleep four. She was the only Kreuger boat built for living onboard.

Match II. *Modern instrumentation blends in with the original steering wheel and brass plate binnacle.*

Match II *was built at Gustavsson & Andersson's yard at Lidingö.*

Left: A roller blind with a tassel was part of the original furnishing detail from 1918.

Littorin named her *Match II* in reference to his industry but "match" can also mean someone's "equal." Or did it refer to the two men's strong partnership? Perhaps the name hints at a competition, as between two teams. *Match II* was used for entertaining ministers of foreign governments and other prominent people, perhaps on a sightseeing trip, at a regatta, or just for a straight business meeting. Littorin sometimes headed out on private trips to the Stockholm archipelago, often to his summerhouse there. The engines on these boats need constant attention. Under the foredeck, there was space for a mechanic and hand who were called in when the engine was having problems. A four cylinder Wisconsin engine with 62 horsepower gave *Match II* a maximum speed of 13 knots. After 10 years, that engine was replaced with a 110 horsepower Sterling B6 which was known for its smooth, vibration-free running. The new engine increased the boat's top speed to 16 knots. Her home mooring was on the pier belonging to the Royal Swedish Motor Yacht Club at Djurgårdsbron in Stockholm.

At the auction in Fittja, the bidding amongst the gentlemen assembled was slow. Finally, Harry Faulkner bought the boat for 14,100 Swedish crowns. He was a director at Separator Inc. which later grew into Alfa Laval, an international engineering company.

Match II remained in the Faulkner family for 30 years. Under later owners, she worked hard as a charter boat and also starred in a Swedish TV show. She could have ended up abandoned on some quayside if it had not been for Solveig and Lars Nygren, two motor yacht enthusiasts from Västervik.

Match II's *quarter-deck. Perhaps this is where the two brothers, Torsten (left) and Ivar Kreuger once sat.*

A motto from Kreuger's and Littorin's time was that a pleasure craft should provide enjoyment and relaxation for her owner. That is still true for the European Motor Yacht Society (MYS) whose members locate and preserve old motor boats. Restoration is carried out in line with the original work, as far as possible. A lot of effort is put in to identifying and preserving historical documentation, drawings, old photographs, and records of previous owners' journeys and adventures.

"Original condition" is a more flexible concept on sea than on land. Since every boat is unique, the MYS guidelines for renovation are fairly generous. The vessel must have been originally constructed for pleasure. New engines and equipment may be installed, including modern aids for piloting and navigation. The external profile should be maintained, or restored if the boat has been modified. Above all, changes must be tasteful and stylish.

When Solveig and Lars Nygren found *Match II* in 1991, the entire transom was missing. Potential buyers were greeted with a large, dark hole. The saloon roof had sunk, the propeller was broken, the rudder post was crooked, and the rudder was askew. The entire covering board, beams, and beam shelves had to be replaced, and the hull needed a lot of work. "Don't buy a wreck! Buy a boat instead!" begged their children.

But Solveig and Lars bought the wreck. They had some idea of what they were letting themselves in for because they had previously restored a large, Norwegian double-ender. This time it was to be a motor boat and it had to be big enough to take three poodles on board.

Now they had found the right shape, size and visual appeal that they wanted. The engine was basically sound, having been used for only four seasons, but needed work. The hull had been stripped of paint and left, so rainwater had discolored it. Yet there was still a beauty about her and that was what was most important. "It's as simple as that," says Solveig.

They decided to try and restore *Match II* to a seaworthy state in the place that they had first found her and so began commuting each weekend between Västervik and Stockholm. Almost every weekend and two years of holidays were spent at the shipyard. Beams and beam shelves were replaced and a new foredeck was laid with oregon pine. The foredeck hatches were corroded by rusty screws and too thin to be salvaged but the skylight glass could be saved. 160 feet of the bottom planking was replaced, a new covering board was laid from stem to stern and the lower saloon walls were also replaced. A new transom with stern frame was fitted. The doors to the afterdeck were too rotten and so new ones were built.

The engineer, Knut Ljungberg (above left) designed the express cruiser Loris *which the silent film stars Douglas Fairbanks and Mary Pickford (above right) had the pleasure of traveling with.*

*The express cruiser
Loris in freshly
restored condition in
the summer of 1998.*

The rudder and propeller were repaired and set true. The modern toilet was replaced by a model which exactly matched the original model, manufactured by Rylander & Asplund. Strangely enough, this was found at a classic car show. A new galley was built—food had previously been prepared on a removable plywood bench on the bridge. Today, there is a gas stove, stainless steel sink, refrigerator, and larder in the new galley. For nostalgic reasons, a piece of fine marble in the galley, from the Kolmård district of Sweden, was saved. Two new mahogany benches were built and fitted along the sides of the bridge. These conceal a waste tank, a gas tank, and other items.

The afterdeck did not need to be replaced; planing and varnishing sufficed. The hull was scraped clean, hundreds of rusty screws and rivets were replaced with stainless steel ones, and old screw holes were plugged with mahogany plugs. The hull was oiled, the bottom was painted with red lead oxide, and the sides were varnished with eight coats.

The mast was shortened slightly because the bottom end was rotting, and new spreaders were made. But *Match II* was still not ready for sea and after two years of work, Solveig and Lars were tired of the long trips to Stockholm. Eventually, she was transported overland to Västervik. The great Kreuter yacht glided south along the main E4 highway. She will be forever remembered pulling in to a gas station in Sörmland.

Early in 1994, the work continued with seaming and sealing the foredeck. The engine was installed and all new fittings were screwed into place. A canopy was ordered for the bridge which needed to be rainproof because cushions were to be placed on the new benches. Cushions were also made for the saloon, curtains for the round saloon windows were sewn, and the fine roller blinds were restored. Instructions in old Swedish still appear on the roller blind control rods.

"Accessories are important," says Solveig who has picked up items at auctions and flea markets. On the wall in the saloon hangs a picture of King Gustav V. The cigarette box, proudly bearing a KSSS emblem (of the Royal Swedish Sailing Society), contains chocolate cigarettes because smoking is not permitted onboard. Authentic china plates and lead crystal glasses are used onboard. Solveij and Lars made the cut glass chandeliers and mahogany frames themselves.

The chest of drawers in the aft saloon was rotting and had some damage caused by damp but has now been thoroughly restored. On the top of the chest, a decorative rail runs all around, incorporating small dolls of mahogany. Solveig and Lars ordered a copy of this work for some new shelves which they fitted in the forecastle. This space had previously been used for the engine but moving the engine back toward the bridge meant that the area under the foredeck could now be used as a captain's cabin.

On July 19, 1994, *Match II* was finally re-launched after having stood on land for six years. Despite the long dry period, she took on very little water. Their resolve, and seemingly their money, never tires. "It has been worth it," feels Solveig. Classic boats have an enthusiastic following and the many encouraging words they receive keep Solveig and Lars on a straight and steady course.

Kreuger's own pennant flies on the jack staff on Loris's bow.

Although the new owner of the motor yacht *Loris* had intended to buy a skerry cruiser, the experience has been similar. *Loris* is long and slim, like a skerry cruiser. She moves through the water with dignity, appearing to lack a maximum speed. The more gas that is applied, the faster she goes.

Loris is a few years older than *Match II* and was the only boat that Ivan Kreuger owned privately. She was ordered in 1913 and designed by the same architect, Knut Ljungberg. Around 20 men worked for three months at the Hästholm shipyard in Stockholm to build her. She was designated an "express cruiser" because she was primarily a fast boat but she also has a small saloon. *Loris* has two cockpits: one is aft of the saloon cabin which also has two bunks, a rest room, and a closet. The large engine is located ahead of the steering position where there is also a small cockpit for the engineer.

Loris was launched in June 1913. Ivar Kreuger wanted a fast boat and that is what he got. A huge 24 liter, six cylinder Sterling Coastguard engine delivering 300 horsepower was installed into the 50 foot lightweight hull. The engine powered *Loris* through the water at the dizzy speed of 27 knots, which was incredibly fast for the time.

Loris was used mainly for trips out to Kreuger's summerhouse in the archipelago but also for entertaining. In the summer of 1924, the silent film stars Mary Pickford and Douglas Fairbanks were going to celebrate midsummer on the isle of Skarpö at the residence of Charles Magnusson—a director of the film studio, Svensk Filmindustri. These celebrities, along with Greta Garbo and the director Mauritz Stiller, were all

For Loris's *deck of South American mahogany, new fittings were cast according to the old designs. Historic photographs of the boat were a big help here. The bitts above were originally* Loris's.

Above: The interior of Loris's saloon.

Opposite: The steering position on Loris. *The instrumentation panel was constructed according to elevator instrumentation of the same period.*

aboard *Loris*. The trip was captured on film by a film maker from Svensk Filmindustri, another piece of Kreuger's empire.

Loris was sold at the same auction as *Match II*. After being owned by a family in Södertälje, she ended up in Copenhagen, Denmark, in the 1960s. *Loris* was sold back to a Swedish buyer but fell into disrepair, sunk,

was then salvaged, and left on land without protection. The boat was vandalized, fittings were removed, and some planking was taken away by unscrupulous boat owners in need of mahogany. She was now rotting and had gaping holes in her planking. *Loris* could well have ended up as firewood. Yet something about her inspired the prospective buyers

Joakim Irebjer, Helena Åberg, and Mats Arrhénborg. Despite everything, she was beautiful.

They bought her without appreciating her history. That *Loris* turned out to be Kreuger's personal motor yacht was an important factor in her fate. The Maritime History Museum of Stockholm certified her value as a piece of cultural history and consequently the Swedish labor department approved her restoration as a re-training project. One of Kreuger's old companies, Hufvudstaden, sponsored the project.

Apprentice boat carpenters from the school at Skeppsholmen did the carpentry. The boat was carefully dismantled and as much as possible of the original timber was saved. The keel timbers and entire underside of *Loris* were replaced. Instead of Honduras mahogany, which is no longer available, highly resinous, slow grown pine heartwood was used here. The timber was quarter sawn to minimize any shifting of the planking. The original deck, which was unusually thin to save weight, had been punctured in several places and could not be saved. Here, South American mahogany was used.

The steel ribs had rusted and so, one by one, they were dismantled, the rust was removed and they were then rebuilt using high-quality steel which was then galvanized. The ribs were attached to the planking using copper rivets which were least likely to corrode.

Original pieces belonging to *Loris* turned up in various places. One day, a man rang to say he had bought *Loris's* original compass and binnacle from an antiques dealer in Copenhagen 30 years earlier. The gentleman

was prepared to part with the compass for the sum he had paid back then.

Other pieces were picked up at antique shops and chandlers. New items were cast according to their original appearance, often on the basis of photographic evidence. *Loris* also had a new motor and electrics.

"You have to convince yourself that it's possible, you have to be stubborn and you must not give up," says Joakim Irebjer. He has worked hard in enlisting the support of many companies who have contributed labor and material. Without sponsors, the project would have been far too expensive for three individuals.

The express cruiser and Kreuger motor yacht, *Loris*, was re-launched in the summer of 1998. The restoration had taken four and a half years and around 25,000 hours of work. Four of the apprentice carpenters now work as full-time boat carpenters.

Loris cuts through her home waters once again, moving stealthily due to the near-silent engine. She smells of the 1920s, albeit with a hint of french fries since her engine is now fuelled by environmentally friendly grapeseed oil. *Loris* is a re-creation of a fine old world: a homage to a romantic ideal. After all, what business leader, with a large sum stashed away, would say no to sipping cocktails onboard a boat like this?

Faster and faster, and still faster when more gas is applied. After four and a half years of restoration work, Helena Åberg, Joakim Irebjer, and Mats Arrhénborg take great pleasure in powering Loris *across her home waters.*

78	**Oden**
⎯	**Double-ended sloop**
38' 9"	length overall
8' 6"	beam
5 long tons	displacement
2' 9"	draft
Ford 2717 E, diesel	engine
Åbo Båtvarf, 1907	place of construction

A rough diamond of the seas

Oden is a double-ended sloop, built in Finland 1907.
Her owner's name is Ulf Selberg but everyone calls
him "Grulf." *Oden* is not for sale but if she were for
sale, the price would be 17 million Swedish crowns
(about $2.5 million). Without really intending to, Ulf
has grown very close to his boat. But that figure is
not plucked out of mid-air. "17 million is how much
another, equivalent boat would cost," explains Grulf
quite earnestly. Gruff arrived at this figure after
simply calculating how much it would cost him to
stop working so that he could spend the rest of his
life building a replica of *Oden*. On the pontoon, Grulf
has assembled what he considers to be essential kit:
a 24-volt generator, an empty red fuel tank, a few
bits of wood, and part of a linen tarpaulin. There is
something a little bit eccentric about Ulf and his boat.
You sense a strong feeling of real work here.

Above: Oden's *steering position is in the open air. The door leads to the fore cabin which also plays the roles of machine room and workshop.*

Many wooden boat lovers put large sums of money and years of work into their passion. They are not satisfied until their boat is in A1 condition with every surface shining like a mirror. That is not the way aboard *Oden* and that is not the way of Grulf.

The boat looks like something out of a costume drama. The beautiful bronze bitts look worn and so do the spindly guard rails which barely seem fit for the purpose. He tried repairing them but it turned out that

they were better left bent so people could see they should not step on them. Could he not have them nickel plated? No, that would be unthinkable! He has also left the old, cast iron bow rail in place, choosing to simply paint it brown.

The mahogany doors leading to the stern cockpit have seen several layers of stain and varnish. Triple-grooved wood trim frames the door panels which are flanked by Jugend period fittings. There is a tension here between a raw, flaking surface and one with air bubbles caught inside the varnish. "I accept this," says Grulf but you can tell that he is not happy about those bubbles. In winter, it will be time to scrape this off. Grulf points out that you should not varnish both sides of the wood because then it will not dry out by the Fall. It's better to give the inside a simple coat of linseed oil, perhaps with some red lead oxide mixed in.

The red-wine colored velvet in the cock pit is showing signs of wear, as though it has never been replaced. It is easy to feel as though you have been whisked back in time to the real, full-blooded 1920s and not to an idealized air-brushed picture of that decade.

There are unusual colors on the boat. The cabin ceiling is almost fluorescent Neapolitan yellow. Outside, the cabin roof is a rich, heavy brown color which smells as though it dates from early last century. "They don't like the color on my cabin roof but I don't understand why it must be white. I don't think there used to be so much white before…"

It is questionable whether the finish on this boat can be called a finish. Grulf and his *Oden* turn the concept on its head. But soon you realize that this is indeed the finish that Grulf wants: it is an expression of human life. It is a finish rich in smells, colors, reflections, and living surfaces. There is a contrast here between old and new.

Oden has been deliberately maintained in a personal way. There is no great strategy at work here, no compulsion to make everything different, just an atmosphere of authenticity that is not found on other boats. The finish speaks of a boat that really has been used and which is still used, of a boat that has had its knocks over the years and which lives on, proud of its history.

In turn, the appearance is a reflection of Ulf Selberg's own philosophy regarding boats: never feel constrained. Working on the boat should be fun. Preparing the boat to sail should be enjoyable.

It is an approach that creates contrasts; differences which draw out a waning beauty;

The compass is built in to the fore cabin.

a beauty that is not fresh and new but one which is experienced, romantic, and slightly nostalgic. It is an atmosphere where you could happily raise a glass, tell each other stories, and laugh together.

Some people are bemused by Grulf. They laugh up their sleeves and talk behind his back. Others are pleased that Grulf and *Oden* are around: his picturesque curiosity makes their own well-polished boats appear to shine even brighter. Still others wonder what Grulf used to varnish his boat. "They ask if I've bought an Indian varnish and painted it on with my beard!" You have to laugh with him...

Perhaps he would like to straighten out a few things but he is largely happy with his boat. Although the trim is a little flaky in places, everything works. Grulf does the maintenance on the Ford diesel engine himself. He has planed the cylinder head and fitted new pistons and valves. He built the hydraulics himself. He knows his boat, all the controls, and instrumentation. If anything goes wrong, he can reach down to the engine and fix it. Grulf is not afraid of new challenges. His father was a blacksmith while he is an engineer, a systems analyst, and a teacher in mathematics and physics.

Like many wooden boat enthusiasts, Grulf is not a stranger to marine carpentry, although he does not do more restoration than is necessary. He would never set about replacing a large area of planking if it was not absolutely necessary. Instead, he would rather splice in smaller pieces where the need is most acute. Perhaps *Oden* will eventually look like a patchwork quilt and maybe he will be teased by others,

*Above: Oden's
aft cockpit looks
particularly inviting
in the sunlight.*

*Left: The interior from
Oden's main saloon.*

but crucially, this approach does not risk replacing the boat's personality. *Oden*'s soul lives on. "I could not care less if other people laugh at me. If I did, I would soon have replaced everything on the boat."

And yet 60 of *Oden*'s 100 oak ribs have been replaced, along with 90 feet of bottom planking in and half a dozen floor timbers. Large areas of the deck and covering board are new. To protect the elongated hull from sinking when it is raised and set down, Grulf has bolted a long iron rail under the keel.

Oden has two saloons—one forward and one aft—with the steering position in between. The saloons are glazed with upright, rectangular panes reminiscent of a horse-drawn carriage. *Oden* has not always looked this way. When she was delivered to her first owner, the open deck between the saloons was 6 feet longer and the stern cabin stretched all the way back to the stern so there was no open cockpit. The boat is sturdily built and tightly ribbed but during the rebuilds, several deck beams have been cut out. The resultant loss of rigidity is causing the hull to widen gradually and that worries Grulf. With all of those roofs, doors, and windows, she leaks a good deal from above. There are many holes to be plugged.

The exposed steering position makes the boat uncomfortable in harsh weather. The helmsman feels the wind and rain. Yet Grulf would never be tempted to build housing for the helmsman. A spray hood and somewhere to keep a chart safe might be acceptable, but no roofing structure.

The boat was built for pleasure trips in Finland's Åboland archipelago. At the end of the 1940s she was bought by a Swede

and taken to Sweden. The KSSS (the Royal Swedish Yacht Club) registered her in 1950. Later, she sank but was soon raised and taken to Stegesund's shipyard. She stayed there, untouched, for close to 25 years. She has never really been sailed in Sweden and does not have much history here. Grulf heard about the boat via a colleague who was considering buying the interior just for its many beautiful fittings. Her hull was grey then but after scraping away some of the paint, it was clear that healthy mahogany was lurking beneath.

Grulf attracted attention early on. *Oden* did not have a working engine and there was a large hole in her bottom. So Grulf fixed the hole as quickly as he could, fitted a two-cylinder outboard engine and slowly puffed out to the island of Björkskär in Stockholm's archipelago with a tarpaulin covering the leaky roof. His dream was to be a sailor; maybe *Oden* could be sailed. The boat has a simple rig but no sail as yet. It would be reassuring if she could be sailed to land in the event of engine failure. Grulf wants to live onboard and he uses the boat for a large part of the year. Many boat owners sleep better onboard than anywhere else but few actually go as far as moving in. Grulf sleeps onboard even when the boat is on land.

Oden can be persuaded to travel at 12 knots but her cruising speed is 8 knots. She is undeterred by big seas and Grulf sails when he has time, no matter what the weather is doing. "I guess they think I'm a little bit crazy but *Oden* is better in the seas than a Pettersson," states Grulf confidently. She has better stern lift and is as stable as a ship.

Oden is the name of the mythical Norse god of war and wisdom. It suits an old boat such as this, a little peevish and patinated. The name is associated with dignity and pride but some of the explanation is simpler still. The boat was originally named Gwen, which is not nearly as grand, but note that the last two letters are the same. This simplified her identity change.

The stern flag is 4 feet long and yet too short for Grulf's taste. "A flag on a sloop like this should be majestic and of king-size proportions." At least another foot, then, even if it has to trail in the water.

Grulf and Oden *head out toward new adventures.*

Sea-Wing	89
Dart racer	

22 ' 2"	length overall
6' 5"	beam
1 long ton	displacement
38 knots	maximum speed
Chevrolet, 235 hp	engine
Toledo, Ohio, USA around 1930	place of construction

Ran	
Forslund racer	

21' 4"	length overall
6' 6"	beam
1.3 long tons	displacement
28 knots	maximum speed
Mercruiser, V8, 260 hp	engine
Östhammar, 1936	place of construction

Faster than a train

Racing across the sea is fun. It fills you with an indescribable rush. Preferably, it should be summer, or a warm fall or late spring—as long as it is not cold or windy and the sea is not rough. Americans understand this. Many are fond of speed, the sound of a hard-working engine, and, of course, fine weather. If it clouds over, you can be home just as quickly as you went out. The similarities with a classic car are striking: a genuine American, muscular V8 and a bench seat behind a chrome-trimmed windshield. With a wooden steering wheel and dazzling fittings and instruments, only a gas pedal and stick shift are missing. The American speedboat *Sea-Wing* and her Swedish cousin *Ran* are runabouts: boats built for racing over calm waters at high speed with the wind blowing in your hair and your sweetheart sitting beside you.

She went on a trip with other racers across the mirror-like waters of Nassafjärden on a warm August day a few years ago. Together with the clear blue sky and a strong front of summer weather, the feeling was unbeatable.

This was cruising at its best: rolling across the water, enjoying the ride, checking out the scene, perhaps going ashore some-where, eating a picnic or popping into a waterside restaurant. Or how about heading out one evening after work, dropping in to Stockholm town before returning at night to the sound of laughter echoing across the water, and the low hum of a far-off engine. You could compare the situation to a meeting of veteran motorcyclists; these racers are not marauding scoundrels. A fine wooden boat can be appreciated from ashore; pedestrians on the promenade at Karlsberg's canal give the boat a thumbs up.

Sea-Wing is a Dart racer, built around 1930 at Toledo, Ohio on the shores of one of the Great Lakes in the north west. Boats were built at the rate of about three a day in the huge factory. An 18 foot mahogany boat with a 60 horsepower Gray engine cost $1,595. The Firm's trademark was the word "Dart" with a dart painted through the middle. These boats competed successfully against other great American boat builders such as Chris Craft and Gar Wood.

Dart was available in four variants. *Sea-Wing's* model name was "The Red Dart" and she was the second boat in terms of size–there being one smaller and two larger models. *Sea-Wing* has three cockpits: one for the driver and his sweetheart, one for the big V8 and one for the mother-in-law furthest back. The frame for the "Red Dart"

was made from the finest ash, oak was used for the keel and ribs, and fine mahogany for the planking. The bottom was made from a double layer of mahogany. The most powerful engine available at the time was a 125 horsepower Chrysler Imperial.

The Dart factory was happy to market their boats through racing. The headlines were hit when a 1929 Dart raced the express train the *Flying Scotsman*, famous for traveling from London to Edinburgh non-stop. The race was to take part along the river Ouse, north of Cambridge, England. The Dart boat won and pictures of the victorious boat were used liberally in marketing brochures. They also turned up in an American boating magazine.

There is much to suggest that *Sea-Wing*

Opposite: Sea-Wing on Lake Alby in 1998.

Below: Race against The Flying Scotsman, 1929. It might have been Sea-Wing who beat the famous stream train.

was the boat that raced the famous express train. "That is probably the case," says *Sea-Wing's* owner diplomatically. Although it is not a certainty, there are several pieces of evidence—including the production serial number—to support the conclusion. Soon afterwards, the boat came to Sweden and the boat's fate there at the time is not known.

Sea-Wing has long, flush decks with a shiny wide stem plate at the bow. Many parts of this boat are shiny, again calling the automobile industry to mind: the bow fitting, fairleads, anti-slip plates, and cleats for attaching fenders are all chromed. The windshield is low and wide and yet it still protects you almost completely from wind. At the bow and stern there are chrome fittings for lifting the boat out of the water making the process straightforward when you have finished your trip. If you drive hard, the boat can begin to leak but after a few hours, it swells again. A jewel like this is not left just anywhere, not unmanned and certainly not uncovered in strong sun. Sunlight bleaches the mahogany, dulls the varnish, and dries out the planking to the point that it can crack. A cover is therefore used frequently.

When the engine is opened up, the wide, flat, buoyant stern almost lifts the whole boat out of the water. Her length means she moves swiftly and calmly through the water. 235 horses and a gallon of gas every 3 nautical miles are needed to keep *Sea-Wing* at her cruising speed of 28 knots. On a fall day with a clear blue sky, she slices through the water like a hot knife through butter.

The mahogany has a deep brown color like tobacco, unlike the more common stained

Above: Sea-Wing
cruising along at 28
knots.

Left: Homeward
bound on a sunny
summer afternoon.

mahogany with a reddish hue. The ribbed mahogany foredeck is a lighter shade with caulked seams. *Sea-Wing* resembles a piece of antique furniture, except that you can water-ski behind this chest.

So how do you get such a brilliant luster? This is how *Sea-Wing*'s owners and carers, Christian and Jeanette Barfod, set about the varnishing: if the surface is already varnished and in good condition, sand it with 260–320 paper. Apply the varnish with a small mohair roller, covering two square foot at a time. It does not matter whether you go with or against the grain. Finally, apply varnish with a paint pad—always in the direction of the grain.

To varnish the whole boat only takes about an hour. The number of coats needed depends largely on your patience. It is important to thoroughly clean all tools before beginning to avoid contaminating the smooth new surface with dust. If you are treating fresh wood, begin planing with 220 paper and then use 180 paper between coats.

The result is magnificent; it is a fine reward for the effort and a clear sign of success. While there is certainly compe-tition to have the shiniest finish, it would be cheating to spray varnish on, says Christian: "That would be treating it like a car."

The keelson is scraped clean every ten years. When the boat is taken up in the fall each year, it is important to remove all of the boat's interior so the inside can be washed and scrubbed clean. Dampness or mold must not be allowed to take hold. Occasionally, a fan is used to thoroughly dry out the hull. Mahogany is sensitive to frost and can crack if it is damp when temperatures reach freezing.

96 *Sea-Wing, Ran*

The Dart was for sale in a newspaper 20 years ago, described as "a racer—type Riva." She was on land but in a poor way, not fully covered and with her fittings lying in a pile inside. The price was 10,000 Swedish crowns in 1983 (about US $1,350 in 1983). The Barfod's pulled up their sleeves and got down to work: planing, scraping, and painting.

You can tire of the work from time to time but there is a cure. She smells good and, "a well cared-for wooden boat is an incredible sight." The Dart is a piece of cultural history and so there is a duty to preserve her for the next generation. When she is in the water and you turn the key... sometimes that is enough bring out tears of joy.

The engine was changed seven years ago. A new one was found via the Yellow Pages. Fortunately, it turned out to be a robust truck block. The piston rings and bottom bracket were changed and the engine was installed. The V8 is a good, simple design and if you need some help, you can always borrow "How to rebuild your smallblock Chevy" at the nearest public library.

Knowing how the engine works provides a sense of confidence, should things go wrong. As a wooden boat owner, it helps if you are multi-talented. *Sea-Wings*'s owners do almost everything themselves: the mechanics, carpentry, sewing, sanding, and surface treatments. They live for their interest almost to the extent that they resent work encroaching on their free time! The Dart is now due for a new cover, which Christian Barfod will sew himself, and a new interior. He built the existing interior and through that he has learnt what could

be done better and how to improve the authenticity. Taking a lead from the original is often the best and most natural-looking solution.

Both *Sea-Wing* and the Forslund racer *Ran* are members of "MYS racers," which is a sub-division of the Motor Yacht Society. According to the Nordic myth, the goddess Ran is the wife of Aegir, the god of the sea. She is notorious for drawing sailors down to her depths. Perhaps relatedly, the Forslund racer *Ran* can be vulnerable to broaching waves, as her owners, Christer Larsson and Bitte Rask, can testify. Swell from large passenger ferries must be taken carefully to avoid waves washing over the whole boat.

It is clear from her lines that *Ran* is a boat from the 1930s. She has a sharp, deep forebody, the freeboards are tall and the boat's occupants have more protection than in the Dart. The Bakelite steering weheel is not original but came from an "Ess" boat, constructed by Gideon Forslund at a shipyard on the Lilla Essingen river in the mid 1930s.

There is plenty of space in the cockpit for up to six people. You cannot sleep onboard, but *Ran* can be a weekend boat if you take a tent with you or stay at a guest house. The Forslund racer is somewhat more Swedish than the racers with American roots. *Ran* does not have a rounded afterdeck, "a barrel back," which is typical of American racing boats. The windshield is taller, providing better protection from the Swedish winds. The bow is a little more splayed and the deck is flatter. Beneath the waterline, the stern is more V-shaped than the flatter Dart.

She is built from mahogany with oak ribs

A classic runabout gets a lot of admiration from the shore.

and a V-bottom hard-chine hull. The boat is tightly ribbed. The hull is strengthened with steel brackets attached to the bilges, and is a single hull design, in contrast to the Dart.

Ran's first owner was a confectioner from Öregrund. When he died in the mid-1970s, *Ran* ended up in a barn where she lay for 15 years before being discovered. She was completely restored to her former glory with new deck beams and a new ribbed deck of Oregon pine. The lower parts of the ribs have been replaced as has a third of the planking beneath the waterline.

Her current owners lack the time and knowledge required to restore a wooden boat but they dearly wanted one because wooden boats feel alive and personal in contrast with fiberglass boats, which are mass-produced according to a standard design.

They bought *Ran* after she had been restored and have since learned much about her care and maintenance needs. Taking a planing machine to the precious, shiny freeboards for the first time felt horrible, but step-by-step things became easier. The varnishing turned out to be particularly complicated. The varnish should be mixed well with a stirring stick but on no account should it be shaken.

That was a mistake that *Ran's* owners made early on but which they will not be repeating. After varnishing the boat's hatches, some of them turned out fine and smooth while bubbles appeared on the surface of others. Could it be because of the temperature? Was it too cold or too hot? The answer was simpler than that: if you shake the varnish tin,

There is something "Swedish" about the Forslund racer.

small bubbles form which then show up on the finished surface.

In contrast to their colleagues with the Dart-racer, they are happy to use a brush for varnishing. The work is slower, the finish ends up being less even and you have to be careful to avoid drips down the freeboards. On the other hand, using a roller has disadvantages too. It is hard to get enough varnish on the roller so the coat can be quite thin. The varnish is applied with brush strokes up and down and from side to side. A paint pad is used in strokes starting from the untreated area, so that there are no breaks or lines across the finished surface.

Many people have their own tips and tricks for varnishing. Some people swear by a particular brand, others mix the varnish in a certain way or dilute it. Varnish from the same manufacturer can vary a great deal; it may be manufactured in Ireland one year and then in Norway the next. The ingredients many change too. Choosing something that you think seems good, carefully reading the directions and then giving it a try, usually gives good results. The degree of success depends more on who is holding the brush than what is in the tin.

Christer Larsson wants his boat to be perfect: *Ran* should be a real head turner. The cockpit is next to be varnished and the next investment is likely to be a cover.

A few years back, a brand new engine was fitted in *Ran*, a Mercruiser V8. There are enthusiasts who are of the view that a new engine does not have a place in an old boat like this but Christer Larsson is of a different opinion: with her new engine the boat feels safer. The reality is that there are

Above: The large V8 engine bubbles and coughs through the exhausts at the transom.

Right: Ran's small deck ventilators are not her original ones. They were fitted by a previous owner.

few boats of this age with original engines. The MYS rules in this area are quite relaxed. It is perfectly acceptable to install a modern, reliable engine along with up-to-date navigation aids if desired.

Even a fairly new engine does not guarantee problem-free running. One day, it did not want to start, producing just a click from the starter motor. It turned out that the solenoid had rusted which was something Christer Larsson could fix himself, happy as he is to carry out routine service and repairs.

When the boat is taken up in the fall, the engine is prepared for its winter break. The cooling system is drained and the pipes are then filled with anti-freeze. This keeps them free of air so that they do not rust. One tip is to remove the thermostat so that it does not close up and prevent the anti-freeze mixture from reaching all parts. Then a little engine oil is poured into the carburetor's air intake and the engine is turned over a few times.

The black Mercruiser looks impressive and sounds great. *Ran* can reach 28 knots now and could probably go faster by changing the angle of the propeller. Currently the engine provides good acceleration but less power is delivered at higher speeds.

Ran is perfect for two people to look after and that is one of her merits. Her maintenance needs are manageable so it is interest levels and enthusiasm that set the boundaries. The time of the year also makes a difference: there is a strong urge to get her shipshape and into the water in early spring.

And what if they needed a larger family boat in the future? Despite everything, *Ran's* owner would still consider a fiberglass boat.

Marie

A Nordic Folkboat

25' 2"	length overall
20'	length at the waterline
7' 3"	beam
260 sq ft	sail area
4 ft	draft
Williams shipyard, Motala, 1959	place of construction

A boat for the people

A common Nordic one-design boat was the vision: a boat
for sailing and competing across national boundaries
on equal terms, made from Scandinavian timber and a
keel of iron. It was the end of the 1930s. War raged in
Europe and Sweden was focused on building a modern
welfare state. Class differences were to be minimized,
the poor were to be helped, and the rich were to share.
Everyone had the right to a decent standard of living.
A boat suitable for all kinds of folk was needed, not an
expensive yacht. Sven Salén, a wharf owner and racing
sailor from Gothenburg, made this suggestion to the
Scandinavian Sailing Organization and a contest was
declared, spanning the Nordic countries. Candidate
designs should be lightweight, ocean-going, cheap to
mass produce, and able to sleep three to four people.
Finally, the construction materials should be sourced
locally to minimize costs.

Above: Marie on a summer's day, Saxar-fjärden, north of Stockholm.
Opposite: A simple and functional rigging was one aim on the Folkboats. There are no spreaders on the mast.

Many designers took up the challenge and 59
entries were submitted to the contest. The
result, however, was anticlimactic: there was
no winner! The panel of judges decided that
none of the entries met all of the critieria.
However, a Nordic Folkboat eventually came
about after a committee refined several of
the contest submissions. The naval architect
Tord Sundén was charged with drawing up
the final design. The first boat was built at
the Arendal shipyard in Gothenburg, being
completed at Christmas of 1941.

The Folkboat caught on immediately with
61 boats being ordered within three months
and over 400 in Sweden after 10 years. The
Folkboat became one of the most popular
racing classes and its reputation spread south
across Europe and to the USA. By the mid
1970s the boat was also being manufactured
in fiberglass. Today there are more than
3,800 Folkboats globally.

One of them is *Marie*, rigged with a S538
sail, she has beautiful orange freeboards.
The secret is larch wood, linseed oil, and
turpentine. Larch wood is similar to pine
with clearly defined annual rings; it gradually
darkens to a reddish color in sunlight. A large
proportion of larch is heartwood, which is rot
resistant, making it ideal for boat building.
Larch shrinks relatively little, is harder and
stronger than pine, is somewhat heavier, and
is more highly regarded.

"The Folkboat looks like a sailboat,"
observes *Marie's* owner, Björn Askerlund.
She sails well in comparison to modern boats
and is also cheaper. "You don't have to be a
bank employee to be able to afford one," says
Björn Askerlund.

Marie's galley and cabin.
Enough room for books and four people—if you want to.

Hence the idea of a low-cost boat for the people still holds true after more than 60 years. *Marie's* owner feels that aesthetics are important for every product, especially when the product is a boat. The Vegan, for example, is a lovely boat, but not as attractive. He adds that he could have bought a Mälar 22'er, a Mälar 30'er or a Scandinavian double-ender, but that the wide choice of Folkboats was the deciding factor.

There are about 1,350 Folkboats to choose from in Sweden. Quite a few have not received the care and attention they deserve—there are gems but they are seldom on the market. It is the poorly kept boats which frequently change hands.

Really well kept boats stand out in the crowd. Quite simply, the boat looks great, is clean and tidy, smells good, and is free of chips and nicks. It is nearly always worth buying a more expensive but better cared-for boat. Repairs have a tendency to take longer and to be more complicated and costly than initially appears. Often it is simply not possible to fully restore a poorly maintained boat. Preserving a good finish is much easier than trying to create one from scratch.

Most wooden boats leak a little as a natural consequence of the boat drying out and shrinking when on land. To declare that a boat does not "leak a drop" is a clear exaggeration. But *Marie* really does not leak much. The planks loosen a little on her first sailing trip of the year, letting in some water. But they soon swell up nicely again.

Marie was built at Williams shipyard in Motala, 1959. The Williams shipyard is legendary for the high quality Folkboats

produced there. Timber is grown naturally and dried correctly and the S538 is built from high quality larch with steamed oak frames. The floor timbers are still fresh after 40 years because of the good care she has received.

Looking after a wooden boat means a lot of work. "About 10 focused days each season," says Björn Askerlund optimistically, before he revises that to a month if you really count all of the time spent on maintenance.

He always makes time for a couple of coats of lacquer as part of the spring preparations. *Marie* does not need to shine like a mirror but a good smooth surface protects the hull from dirt, splashes, and pollutants. Many people believe that a boat looks its best when just varnished, as long as the wood is beautiful. It is common to see painted freeboards on older boats, sometimes

Marie needs both wind and waves to be at her best. Then she sails brilliantly.

hiding damaged or discolored wood which the owner has given up on. Painted freeboards are also commonplace because they were fashionable on Folkboats in the past, particularly in bold and striking colors.

Marie's planking was varnished internally but Björn has scraped that off. Wood does not fare well when its pores are shut on both sides; the damp needs a way to escape and then re-enter as the humidity levels vary with the weather and the seasons. Instead of varnish, Björn uses a particular type of oil, which is similar to varnish but softer. He also uses this on spars, "but it has to be diluted," he adds.

If the hull needs to be scraped clean, then 10 days of work are not enough: double that is closer to the mark. When the boat is free of varnish, the hull is drenched in linseed oil diluted with turpentine, both inside and out.

Caring for *Marie* in this way does not feel like a burden. Rather, it is exciting to take her up in the Fall, scrub her clean and plan the year's work. Some things need to be done in November or December, such as scraping and oiling, so the oil can dry for a few months before treating other surfaces.

Fingers get twitchy. You can try things out for yourself if you want to, which is rewarding; perhaps change the interior a little, buy a piece of mahogany, shape it and fit it… Over the years, your experience and knowledge of caring for the wood grows. Lessons from woodworking classes in school come back to life as you learn about different sorts of wood and treatment methods. There are always people to ask in the boat club and sometimes you meet a

professional boat builder who you can learn a lot from just by watching. Another source of tips is of course chatting with other club members.

The idea behind the Folkboat was low-price, simplicity, good sailing qualities, and a strict one-design boat. The intention was not to come up with a particularly fast boat and the Folkboat dawdles in light wind. It is important to maintain pace by using the right technique. Avoid steering too high in to the wind when beating because otherwise the hull slows up quickly and awakening her again is tough. Keep an eye on the burgee and watch how the winds twist and turn. In winds of 20-25 feet per second she sails perfectly.

The Folkboat's standing rigging is both simple and unusual. There are no spreaders so the mainsail does not wear so much on a run. The shrouds do not go to the top of the mast; instead there is a jumper stay, which steadies the mast at the top.

The Folkboat has survived in part because it has kept pace with the development of sails and equipment. Almost every year, there is a change to the class rules to keep it a good one-design boat. There are few rules concerning those factors which do not influence the boat's speed; the cockpit and cabin interior can be designed freely. The mast is anchored to the keel timbers in older boats but has been moved up on deck in modern boats to provide more room in the cabin.

The boat can be raced along the entire length of the Swedish coast in small regattas or in larger international meetings. The Folkboat class is still raced actively and *Marie*'s previous owner sailed in the Swedish championships. Björn Askerlund does not race himself but uses her for day trips and sleepovers in Stockholm's archipelago. The Folkboat draws 4 feet, which is less than many modern sailboats. You can venture into small bays and other places where others dare not moor.

The space inside takes some getting used to. You cannot stand, as in most modern boats, but must learn to move in a way that works. A boom cover that stretches over the whole cockpit extends the available living area. Best of all is the proximity to the water. "When you are so close to the water that you can dip your hand in, you feel more at one with the sea." Boats and the sea give a sense of freedom and independence which becomes more important when you are stuck in the rat race of everyday life. At sea you decide your own pace and a wooden boat intensifies the feeling. A wooden boats blends with nature, it is built from materials found on the islands around you. The wooden boat challenges your skills, puts you to the test, gives you new experiences, and allows your knowledge grow.

But where do you find the time? "You have to take time," says Björn Askerlund knowingly. It is a matter of priorities. Life is not all about work and you do not get a second try at it.

Folkboats of the highest quality were built at Williams yard in Motala.

Korall

The Solö cabin boat

23' 10"	length overall
7' 5"	beam
1 long ton	displacement
17 knots	speed
Volvo BB 70	engine
Einar Runius	constructor
Storebro, 1951-64	place of construction

The Electrolux boat

Archipelago boat S 10 M

16' 9" / 17' 3" / 17' 9"	length overall
5' 7"	beam
Storebro, 1947–52	place of construction

The archipelago's automobiles

She could be described as an automobile for Stockholm's archipelago, designed for pleasure. She is a robust day-cruiser with sporty lines, powered by a Volvo engine. Her open cockpit invites you to enjoy the journey with the wind in your hair. The Solö was luxuriously exclusive; costing considerably more than an automobile, she was beyond the reach of the average man. The price tag was 18 months of an industry worker's wages. The story of Solö begins at the end of the Second World War. Many inhabitants of the Baltic countries fled their homes when the Soviet Union's Red Army invaded from the east. Estonians took to small fishing and rowing boats to cross the Baltic. Some landed in Storebro in Sweden, a small industrial town, where they found work manufacturing tool machines. In an old barn, they built boats in their spare time, just as they had done back home.

Above: One Volvo for the road and one for the sea. Ready-made Solös in a row outside the yard in Storebro, sometime during the 1960s.

Opposite: A fun and fancy life onboard and onshore. The advertising for the Solö and the smaller Vindö was American style.

The visionary new factory director Ivar Gustafsson realized that the boat refugees could be valuable to Storebro and, over time, Sweden's most successful luxury boat business came to fruition.

The Solö is one of the first of a whole range of classic pleasure boats built at Storebro. For 13 years from 1951, the original Solö was built, the "Solö Ruff." She was a flush-decked cabin boat with portlights built in to the planking under the large foredeck. The Estonian craftworkers stood for traditional boat building and skillful craftmanship. The Solö was also sold semi-assembled for the self-builder. The purchaser received a completed hull with ribs and planking while the deck and superstructure were delivered in pieces, which the owner then had to assemble.

Solö's designer was Einar Runius, a pupil of the famous Swedish boat builder C.G. Pettersson. Runius's goal was to design an open boat suitable for day trips and transportation with a generous cockpit and a cabin under the foredeck. The hull had a V-shaped bottom and rounded bilges. This 1950s Swedish day cruiser was fast—reaching 18 knots—and the convenient cabin made it ideal for sunny weekend trips. You could spend a night away just by crawling into the cabin under the foredeck.

If you look carefully, the Pettersson ancestry is quite clear. The concept of a cabin under the foredeck and a large cockpit astern is a direct inheritance, although the hull is considerably wider. Earlier designers had opted for relatively narrow hulls which suited heavy, low-revving engines. Now though, engines were stronger and capable

of propelling wider hulls. A converted Volvo B16 was often installed in Solö boats, which is the same engine that was developed for the Volvo automobile, the PV 444.

Today the Solö is much sought after by veteran boat enthusiasts. Over 1,000 wooden examples were built but it is tough to find a well-kept example from the 1950s or 60s. Many boats have been rebuilt or modernized over the years. "There might be only 500-600 left now," says Anders Jelving who, together with Anna Blomberg, owns the *Korall*, a Solö built in Storebro in 1964.

They have put almost 3,000 hours into their boat. Anders has counted them by carving a small groove into his rear shed for every hour completed. *Korall* has production number 932 and she was the perfect basis for a restoration project with her faded, flaking hull. No major wood work has been undertaken; the only wood being replaced

was a strip of rail. The bottom was scraped clean and red lead oxide applied in the traditional manner. The hull was varnished and the mahogany stained to bring out the deep bronze color. Today she looks as though she has just been delivered from the Storebro yard, 40 years late. The dashboard with rev counter and instruments for oil pressure and engine temperature are all original, as is the mahogany boat hook.

Restoring *Korall* has not incurred huge costs beyond that of sandpaper, paint, and varnish. Admittedly, the fittings were chromed and chroming is expensive but time has been the biggest input. Anders and Anna take *Korall* out as often as they can, clocking up 600–700 nautical miles in a season, much of it in the evenings and weekends. They enjoy taking part in veteran boat regattas, happily wearing a skipper's cap with aplomb. Such meetings act as a spur to those who have started out on their restoration work and inspire others in the right direction.

In a genuine Solö there is a strong wooden boat sensation with plenty of varnished mahogany. Mahogany is a good wood for boat building because it is resistant to rot and temperature changes and gives relatively little. It is durable but also quite brittle depending on the quality. It is usually named according to its country of origin. The finest is Honduran mahogany which has a deep red color but is now very rare. African mahogany is of a lower quality, being softer than American and more sensitive to frost. The growth of African mahogany is less regular, leading to a proliferation of end fibers which can cause moisture to be taken up in unexpected places.

Above: Paddle and boat hook within easy reach along the planking.

Opposite: The steering position on Korall. The dashboard is from 1964.

The Solö has a clinker-built hull of
African or Brazilian mahogany on an oak
frame. She is best taken up well before
winter so she can dry out properly before the
onset of frost. When on land, it is advisable
to dry every clinker with a rag and air the
boat thoroughly, opening doors and hatches,
ensuring that condensation does not form.
The moisture has to be released to ensure
that the planking does not crack when
the frost comes. Any obvious penetration
by moisture should be scraped down,
particularly along the garboard strake and
the bows.

The deck on a Solö boat was made from
Oregon pine with a layer of masonite to keep
it water-tight and the cabin sole was made
from solid mahogany. The galley stowage
may have either drawers or cupboards.
Sometimes there are round portholes while
other examples have square panes. The
cockpit is large and open, accommodating
up to 8 people with no significant sinkage.
The large Oregon pine deck is reliably tight,
as is the windshield. Some disadvantages are
that the boat can get quite wet from rain and
splashes and there is a lack of stowage for
lines and anchors.

Korall's engine, a Volvo BB70, is polished
and clean. The rubber engine mounts
minimize vibrations in the hull. The
electrics and carburetor have been replaced
and new fuel pipes installed. At a cruising
speed of 12-13 knots, *Korall* consumes less
than a fifth of a gallon per nautical mile. Her
top speed is 17 knots.

The Solö was modified several times
before finally disappearing from production
in 1977. An older variant of the Solö was 8

*Above: The ventilator
and the cleat on the
foredeck are both of the
famous Solö model.*

*Left: Korall's cruising
speed is 12 knots. The
stern is broad and the
engine gives the boat a
powerful push.*

inches shorter and a foot narrower. Although the hull was widened and lengthened, and the boat had a new interior, it was still built entirely from wood. In 1968, the Solö took its first steps into the world of fiberglass. The hull had grown to 25 feet by 8 feet 6 inches. The hand-built fiberglass hull was still married to a wooden interior. The boat became an increasingly luxurious craft, justifying the addition of the word "luxury" to the boat's name. The old, open-cockpit day cruiser had grown up to become a comfortable luxury craft.

The Solö was built on the floor of the Storebro yard, with many units being assembled simultaneously, like a small production line. For Sweden, this was a completely new approach to boat building, as boats were previously custom-built, one-by-one, according to individual instructions. Storebro pioneered mass-production a few years earlier because the Solö was a replacement for an overnight cruiser, "the Electrolux boat." The Electrolux boat was a small, practical boat built for day trips out to the archipelago. She was a boat for getting out and about in, for enjoying the fresh air and sunshine.

The Electrolux Company was a large, famous manufacturer of outboard motors in the mid-1940s. Sweden was a world leader in the outboard motor industry and Electrolux had just bought the Swedish manufacturers, Archimedes and Penta. Outboards were a major Swedish export product and were sold in large quantities to developing countries. They were robust, low-revving, and powerful. The design, consisting of a free-spinning flywheel and opposed cylinder, had

its roots in the 1920s.

During the Second World War, Electrolux manufactured outboard motors for the Army. When the war ended, there was a surplus of unsold stock. The company management realized that they would not be able to sell them all, at least not without boats to go with them. So they decided to sell a complete package consisting of an outboard motor with a small boat. Several shipyards and boat builders produced boats for Electrolux. Storebro became one of the suppliers in 1947.

The boat's official name was the "Archipelago S-10M" but it was commonly referred to as the *Electrolux boat*. She was clinker-built from mahogany on a steamed oak frame. Overall lengths available were 16' 9", 17' 3", or 17' 9", all with a beam of 5' 7". A 12 horsepower Archimedes B–22 on the transom gave a topspeed of around 10 knots.

Electrolux negotiated down the prices of their suppliers and rationalized the production process. This was true mass-production. The Estonian boat builders worked on the planking of six boats at a time while the interior was built simultaneously on six other completed hulls.

These small camping boats were very popular as testified by the ship merchant Gösta Berg in Stockholm. He wanted to order a further 200 boats but Storebro had to decline the request because Electrolux had already ordered so many. Around 1,500 Electrolux boats were built at Storebro between 1947 and 1952.

Private boat owners had different demands from the Estonian boat builders. The original priorities were robustness and

seaworthiness. Later, the appearance became more important than safety or durability. A boat's finish was a key area of competition. A professional boat builder would evaluate the boat's lines to determine how the hull would perform at sea. In contrast, a private buyer looked more at the exterior, at the seductive bronze mahogany, and the dazzle of the finish.

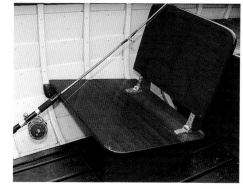

A boat for fishing and camping—complete with an engine—the Electrolux boat.

The Duckling

22' 1"	length overall
6 ft	beam
0.87 long tons	displacement
150 sq ft	sail area
2' 7"	draft
Thorvald Gjerdrum	constructor
Orust, 1998	place of construction

A Stradivarius in the waves

You do not have to love dungarees to own a wooden boat. You do not have to be eager to leap onboard with a saw and plane or varnish and sandpaper. Simply owning a wooden boat, enjoying her and sailing her can be enough. That describes Bengt Braun, the happy owner of a small sailboat made from mahogany and oak.

"A year ago I was in Marstrand meeting a good friend and we were just about to climb aboard his small motorboat when I caught sight of a small mahogany sailboat. I just stared and thought the lines were absolutely fantastic and wondered, what is this?" 'It's a Duckling class,' he said, 'and it's mine.'

"So we waited a while then he lifted off the cover and then those fantastic smells hit me..."

It was love at first sight. Bengt Braun had been charmed. Indeed, he fell in love with the Duckling.

He says the feeling was indescribable. It was the craftsmanship, the lines, the quality; altogether it brought love to life. He made a quick decision and then a few telephone calls to Larsson's shipyard. After having seen some color photographs, Bengt Braun ordered his boat.

Can you buy a boat simply because it is beautiful? Yes, Bengt Braun can. The price seemed reasonable but was in fact unimportant, he adds.

She was so incredibly elegant with her well-balanced proportions and provocative duck-like rear end. Carvel-built, mahogany craftsmanship with painstakingly well-thought out and executed solutions. The deck fittings are made from ash just like the frame. The planking is screwed together from the outside, which makes the frames fine and smooth on the inside. The mast is made from Oregon pine and a long garboard strake of oak forms a base for the fin keel.

Originally, Bengt Braun was planning on something quite different: a fiberglass boat, which could be thrown into the water for a quick sail to his summerhouse. He ended up with precisely what he was trying to avoid!

Then he talks at length about the happy times with the Duckling and about the surprise and happiness when he found out how she behaved at sea. Slightly underrigged perhaps but a total sailing experience. "She is so wonderful you barely want to put her in the water…"

Some say that size doesn't matter but in this context that must be wrong. In the eyes of many, Bengt Braun is a big man. He is tall, a successful businessman, a man whose name commands respect in many boardrooms.

He is educated and is not of insignificant means. Money is not his biggest concern when he decides to buy a pleasure craft. He could have chosen to invest in a considerably larger, more luxurious, higher status boat.

But Bengt Braun has not done that. Instead he is a big man in a small boat. In this little wooden boat, everything is much more fun and much simpler. Things happen faster and the experience is greater.

The Duckling is stiff even though she is small. She responds well to the seas and feels like a real boat despite her size. The proximity to water enriches the sailing experience. You can sail through channels and drop anchor in bays which larger boats would not dare attempt.

Long and drawn-out preparatory work is not necessary. The distance between thought and action is short. Do I want to sail today? 15 minutes after the impulse and you are in the water and away. The upshot of this is that sailing outings are more frequent and the experience is more exhilarating. Closeness to water and the vulnerability of being in a small boat heighten the sensation.

Once the umbilical cord is cut, you are completely focussed on the sea, the boat, and the surroundings, in total concentration. Being so close to the sea contributes significantly to the experience. With the cover down, you feel the wind in your face. When you drop your arms from the rail, water ripples between your fingers. Contact

with nature is a big part of the wooden boat experience; everything feels closer when you are surrounded by the sea, the heavens and islands. This little boat encourages you to take her out and sleep over on a skerry somewhere. There you notice she is in touch with her environment. She is made from natural products and so she has an ecological relationship to nature.

The difference between fiberglass boats and wooden boats is analogous to the difference between fast food and home-cooked food, philosophizes Bengt Braun. Or you could compare the wooden boat experience with fine wines. Expectations run high and with time you learn to how to appreciate it.

The planking is screwed in to the ribs from the outside, which results in a completely smooth inside.

Above: Simple,
functional and
elegant carpentry
in the cockpit.

Right: Sailing
may not be quite
necessary but
it is certainly
wonderful.

After the first outing, Bengt rang the boat builder, Ante Larsson, and told him all about the experience, which was much appreciated.

The Duckling is a piece of art, claims Bengt Braun, both in body and in soul. It is a joy just to have her and a pleasure to look at her. "Every morning, the first thing I do is go outside down to the jetty just for the thrill of seeing her there," says Bengt. It is not the the the boat's monetary value that means the most. Instead, just like other works of art, it is the fact that another human being has applied his soul, his professional knowledge, and his experience to this creation.

"And all on something to bring joy to *me*!" exclaims Bengt.

The boat builder, Ante Larsson, lives in Kungsviken on Sweden's west coast. He is a humble and calm-voiced person who points to his father as his teacher. Experience, tradition and accuracy are found in every detail of the finished boat; the cockpit's softly rounded coaming and barely perceptible tilt; the form of a knee in the cockpit or a cleat on the foredeck. Throughout the course of his professional life, Ante Larsson has learnt about boat building, day-by-day. With the foundation of his solid experience, he can spend time developing new methods and experimenting a little. The Duckling is in a constant state of development and today's Duckling is subtly different from the first which were built at Larsson's shipyard.

"Respect for the person who built this grows as you come to the realization that you could never manage such a feat yourself," says Bengt Braun.

Bengt Braun's father built violins so he knows something about the work that can lay hidden inside a piece of craftmanship. Just like an old violin or antique furniture, the Duckling instills a sense of eternity.

"I have a Stradivarius for a boat," he chuckles. Bengt Braun belongs to perhaps the most distinguished of wooden boat lovers. He cultivates his interest in wooden boats and his Duckling as others enjoy a work of art. The Duckling needs care and attention but he hands that work over to those who have the necessary knowledge and skills, leaving him free to get as much as possible out of sailing the Duckling each season.

To attempt the preparatory work would feel wrong. You do not take sand paper to a Stradivarius if you do not know what you are doing. He hands this over to the experts, then stands aside and observes, as if at an art museum. He has great respect for the profession and its traditions.

"I don't like stripped wood furniture. If you can avoid changing an original, you should. The boat should stay as it was originally conceived."

He allows no argument here. He respects the boat builder, the artist. Even if you felt there was something missing in da Vinci's *Mona Lisa*, you would not take out a brush and start painting it in. The argument says a lot about how valuable this wooden boat is, and how much more it will become in the future.

Around 100 Ducklings have been built. Tore and Ante Larsson in Kungsviken have built most of the Swedish boats.

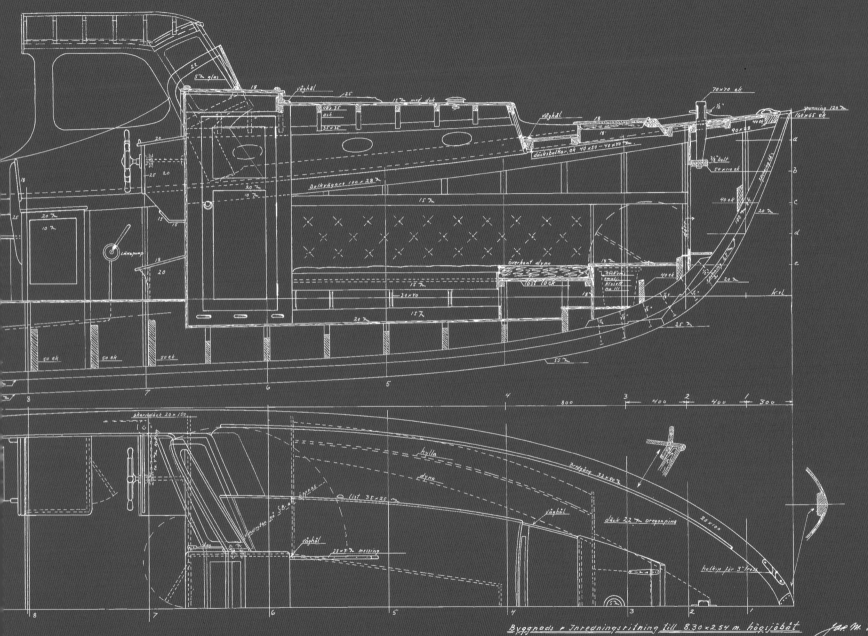

Byggnads- r Inredningsritning till 8.30 × 2.54 m. högsjöbåt

From keel timber to bow fitting

Building a new wooden boat demands a lot of patience. Care and experience is required in the selection of materials, the type of wood, and appropriate methods. Most of all, it demands time. This boat is a 27 x 6 foot high seas boat with a buoyant, double-ended stern. She is part working boat, part leisure boat and is being built at Wätö boatyard by Johan Månsson and his companions.

Although the boat is new, the design is old, dating from 1938. The architect was Jac M. Iversen, a major contributor to the modern Swedish leisure fleet. Iversen was a traditionalist with new ideas and the inspiration for this boat came from the double-ended fishing and working boats built along the Swedish and Norwegian coasts for hundreds of years. In contrast to farmers and fishermen, people on leisure cruises did not need low freeboards to pull in nets or load cargos on to their boats. They also chose to abandon the option of sailing or rowing and put their trust in the boat's engine. This motor boat was only to be used for recreational purposes and so the demands for comfort increased.

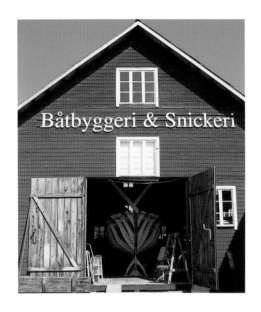  

1] Work starts in the old shipyard at the end of summer in 1996. The bows have been lifted and the molds are in place.

2] The hull's shape is determined by molds, which are attached with precisely spaced laths. The molds are removed when the planking is complete. The curves must be even to allow the lines to merge together as smoothly as possible.

3] The planking is built up on alternative sides, starting from the keel timber. Riveting is a two man job, with one person using a ball peen hammer on the inside, while the other holds a backing iron against the rivet on the outside.

The constructor added a modernizing feature, the extended bow, which appeared on motor boats twenty years later and on modern semi-planing motor boats. The stern is conventional for a double-ender but the bow is broader to protect from splashes and waves. Consequently, the foredeck is as big as on modern motor cruisers. The first example of the design was ordered by a factory owner on Sweden's west coast with a further boat being built later, in 1946. That, it appeared, would be the end of the line.

Nevertheless, fifty years later a third boat is being built according to the same design. The keel timbers are placed on the floor in the workshop and Pär Wahlgren helps shipbuilder Månsson to raise the bows of the boat. Using the drawing as their guide, they attach full scale molds with the help of thin laths evenly spaced along the keel. The molds have to be in line to ensure that the curves of the boat are smooth and match the drawing exactly, to give the lines a beautiful symmetry.

The keel timbers are treated with red lead powder blended with linseed oil, a poisonous mixture that gives good protection against rot. Planking starts from the bottom with planks being added in turn on each side. The boat is clinker built. Planks are pressed against the molds and fastened with long copper rivets. Riveting is a two-man job: one man works on the inside and the other pushes against the rivet on the outside. If the planks need lengthening they are placed with their ends together and a block is fastened over the seam on the inside. There are technical recommendations of how close these butt blocks can be fitted; some planking timbers are 20 feet long.

The oak planks need to be twisted and turned in many ways and the wood puts up strong

resistance. At the sternpost, the double twist becomes especially apparent. The wooden pieces have to fit exactly into the rabbet of the keel and bow. Each planking timber is then riveted against the one below, until the gunwale is reached. It is not until then that the boat builders know if the sheer will pass the test, if it matches with the drawing and if they themselves will feel happy with it.

When the planking is finished there is no more need for the molds. They are removed and it is time to start fitting the wooden interior. The floor timbers are put in place and bolted to the keel. The first boards are screwed tightly against the floor timbers, which also makes the hull more stable.

The big hull, made from dense oak boards, trembles without a frame, moving like a boneless fish in water. It is time to add the ribs. The material is carefully chosen oak, profile routed, 1 ¼ x 1 ⅝ inch, that has been submerged in water for 14 days. They are now soaked and will be steamed at a temperature of 175° F for 25 minutes, until they are as soft and pliable as possible. If left too long, the water evaporates and the wood becomes brittle. A rule of thumb is 25 minutes per inch.

Water drips from the workshop's heating drum. It is fuming hot and the ribs are still steaming when Pär Wahlgren comes running into the workshop with them. Johan Månsson uses his full body weight to force the ribs inside the planking, where they are nailed from the outside. The boat builder's fingers are frozen, their breath rises and they groan under the strain of the hard work.

The oak boards are strong, hard, durable, and now water repellent. The wood smells strongly of tannic acid. Most of the oak comes from the island of Orust, but a smaller consignment is from the area around Arboga. Not all of it can be used; it is hard to get hold of good raw material. Some of

4] The planks are added layer by layer. The planking boards are steamed and then kept in place by clamps. They are riveted to each other using copper rivets that go all the way through the wood.

5] The oak needs to be twisted and turned in all sorts of ways. The curves become most noticeable at the sternpost. Each piece of wood has to fit exactly into the rabbet.

6] The planking is complete and it is time to start on the ribs. The wood has been soaked for two weeks and then steamed for 20 minutes.

7] Fitting the ribs is hard work but has to be done fast. While the wood is hot it is easier to bend, but it soon stiffens.

the wood cracks despite careful drying. On occasion, as much as half of the purchased consignment is rejected, but, on the other hand, the remaining wood is almost completely free from of knots.

The thin drills for the rivets measure $\frac{1}{8}$ inch and they constantly snap. The builders follow the drawings to every detail, where instructions for all dimensions are laid out. Iversen was very careful, stating the exact measures between each screw.

They do, however, allow themselves some additions of their own. The most obvious one is the big doghouse, which is inspired by Iversen's considerably smaller version. The lines have been extended towards the stern to allow more standing space whilst steering, and better protection from splashes and wind. The demands for comfort are indeed higher today than at the end of the 1930s.

The spacious cockpit can fit up to eight people so making the foot boards from compact teak, which was Iversen's recommendation, seems unreasonably expensive today. Pine is used instead.

Changes to the original interior design include replacing the enamel Kockum's toilet, model 111, with a modern toilet and tank. In the galley, there is now standing room, and an oven is installed under the doghouse to the starboard side. The cabin is fitted with water-filled radiators and is aired by solar-powered ventilators. The steering position is placed to port.

To set about building a wooden boat on this scale is a huge challenge. The construction phase is tricky and it is a huge satisfaction just to be able to complete it. The wooden boat builders of today are even more careful than those of the 1930s. New joining techniques, adhesives, and materials have been developed. Brass screws have been replaced by corrosion-free screws. It is not easy to

glue oak, but a modern polyuretan glue is tough enough for the job. The deck seams are better: a rubber strip at the bottom with sealant up to the top fills them up snugly and makes the wooden deck water tight.

Boat builders prefer completely knot-free wood for the hull. But this is a utopia; there are hardly any completely knot-free boats. The boards for the cabin sides are from the same oak tree, which lends a kind of symmetry and visual harmony, although this fact might be lost on those not in the know. The sides of the doghouse are beautifully dovetailed. The beams in the cabin roof are chosen from a trunk with natural bends, which is far superior to having sawed or glued beams.

Just for the the deck and cabin, Johan Månsson has cut about 60 dovetails by hand, which is both difficult and time consuming. At the same time there is room for new ideas and more creativity. The bottom of the toe rail has been given a lip to keep running water off the topsides, which will prevent discoloring, and possibly even decay, in the planking in years to come.

Most fittings, like the bow fitting and the keel bar, are made of stainless steel. A factory in Skultuna has cast new Iversen bollards in chromate brass according to the old model. Iversen took great interest in the fittings on his boats and the inspiration for this one came from Finland.

Building this boat is a way of stretching and proving their own skills. With a hint of regret, Johan reflects that, "craftmanship doesn't suit our times." The hourly rate is low and the work is slow. There are many factors that play a part. The humidity in the air makes a difference and the wood has to dry slowly. You could question whether it is practical and economically viable to build such

8] The deck beams at the stern are in place. The angle between the top planking and the beam shelves needs to be planed, in order to give the deck its proper line.

9] The cabin sides are fitted together. The sides of the cabin and doghouse are carefully dovetailed.

10] The deck is made of Oregon pine, a light, resinous type of wood with a yellow sheen. The seams are caulked with neoprene rubber strips at the bottom and then topped up with an elastic rubber composition.

11] The deck boards are attached to the deck beams.

a big wooden boat today. But this is exactly what makes it special; no trouble is too great and they look for the utmost quality in every detail. "You can't build any faster than this," Johan says with a laconic smile.

The high sea double-ender should have been launched in the summer, but a year later she is still in the yard. Deck beams, deck boards, and cabin sides are in place. She looks more impressive than ever and consumes almost the entire workshop now.

The amber-colored deck is made of Oregon pine, which has similar qualities to Swedish pine heartwood. The deck boards are put into place in the old fashioned way, without any bends and parallel with the fore-and-aft line. Avoiding cuts into the king plank makes it more attractive, claims the boat builder. The cockpit is an open saloon, where you will be able to sit at arm's length from the sea. With two extendable tables, there will be enough room for a small crowd.

The project is running late. It proved harder than expected to adapt an old design to modern standards. The boat might look almost finished but there is a lot left to do down below: bunks have to be fitted, and seats and stowage places organized in the cockpit. Fitting the engine, steering, and rudder also remains, and ends up taking longer than anticipated. The building of the hull and deck went relatively fast, but the changes to the design in the superstructure impeded progress.

A modern leisure boat demands all sorts of additions and safety features that neither existed nor were deemed necessary at the end of the 1930s. Safety aspects and rules regarding the installation of fuel systems and cookers make things complicated. The flushing toilet in the fore cabin makes it

necessary to redesign the whole front cabin. The boat builders are forced to try out new ideas, build models, make their own drawings, adjust, and rethink, before they find the best solution.

Controls and instruments are fitted. The boat will have double, extra large fuel tanks which must be placed centrally and as low as possible to avoid adversely affecting the centre of gravity. The solution is to place them under the seats on each side of the companionway. The galley under the doghouse, with a cooker, running water, and waste disposal, is designed and constructed from scratch. The same goes for the drawers by the steering position and the cupboards for crockery.

Even at this stage, the key is more haste, less speed. Time is needed to make sure every solution works. If you are building an anchor box for a Bruce anchor you need to stow the anchor several times to see if the box really works. Lockers for the fenders are constructed and built in the same way, using the fenders themselves as models—paper plans do not always work in practice.

The bollards, made of cast, chromate brass, are screwed into place. The bow fitting, bow pulpit, bow rail, and bumper guard are screwed into place. The table and cool boxes are installed.

Inboard, the hull is treated with linseed oil, terpentine balsam, linseed paint, and red lead powder. Externally, the hull is treated with Owatrol. It is necessary to apply 35 coats of the base oil within a 48 hour period. Then a surface oil is added which creates a water repellent effect and gives the outside an almost varnish-like finish. The oil makes the boat easier to maintain and longer lasting. The impregnation process is decisive: the oil must be applied in the right manner and at the right level of humidity in order for the oak to be completely soaked through.

12] Work on the afterdeck has begun. The covering boards are in place, as is the king plank which is made of oak.

13] The outside of the hull is carefully polished and then treated with 35 layers of base coat. Treating the boat with Owatrol makes it easier to maintain. You only need to clean, sand, and apply new varnish each year. "You'll propably need to spend about twenty to thirty hours a year to keep her in good condition," says the builder after giving it some thought.

14] A few final layers of oil on top of the base coat gives a finish that is as shiny as varnish.

15] Playing with the positioning of the carved name plate is a pleasure too hard to resist.

16] The large windows along the front of the cabin allow a lot of light in.

If the treatment is done incorrectly, the wood begins to dry out after a couple of years. Moisture creeps in, which makes the wood expand, crack, and then dry again. Decomposition has started.

The hull looks almost varnished now and the planking has a matte silk surface. The bottom has been oiled, given a layer of primer, and finally painted with bottom paint.

At last, the day of the launch has come. It is almost two years since the keel was laid and now it is time for a test drive. It hardly comes as a surprise that Iversen's double-ender is an excellent boat at sea, well equipped for strong winds and rough seas. The hull ploughs effortlessly through strong head sea and in a tailwind, she raises a little and surfs on the waves. She is easy to maneuver and steer, with the exception of reversing. A long keel holds the double-ender steady on her course, but makes it impossible to reverse to port, like other boats of a similar design. This Vätö-designed double-ender is proof that the old constructions still work—with their pros and cons.

There is enough room to stand in the doghouse by the steering position, and the protection from wind and weather is good, even though the lines of the exterior are a point of discussion. The big propeller grabs hold of the sea and pushes the hull forward at a resolute speed of 6.5 knots. The laws of nature prevent any faster speed than this. The maximum speed of a displacement boat can be calculated from its length at the waterline. The double-ender is crank when not in motion but the stern is broad and buoyant, and it quickly steadies her when you accelerate. As the speed increases, her crankiness disappears completely.

The entry into the cabin is a bit low, but inside it is light and roomy. A big double window along

the front edge of the cabin side lets in lots of light and gives a feeling of space and comfort onboard. The berths are long and comfortable. The texture of the wood and its symmetrically arranged grain is nothing short of art: just the sight of it is uplifting. Part of the interior has been painted with a linseed oil paint, which gives off a wonderful smell and a vivid, matte shine.

The galley is properly equipped with an oven and two sinks under the doghouse. Two cool boxes have been installed in the cockpit, and drawers for cutlery and such things are found to port, behind the steering position. There are big, ventilated stowage areas under the thwarts in the cockpit.

The boat suits both day trips and overnight stays for two people. But the best part is the magnificent cockpit, spacious enough for eight people. It confirms the view that it is the journey that is the real joy.

This Iversen-designed double-ender from Vätö is an orgy of fine craftmanship. Now she is launched, but is she finished? No, it will take a few more years yet. From experience, the boat builders know that even after the hull has been completed, a lot of work remains: completing the interior furnishings, the fittings, electrical systems, and navigation aids; installing the engine, and other features. How much time it takes depends on the owner's demands.

The Owatrol treatment makes the boat easy to maintain and you should only need to clean, sand, and varnish a little every year. "You'll propably need to spend 20–30 hours a year to keep her in good condition," says the builder after giving it some thought.

And finally one small detail: in the stern wall of the cockpit are two symmetrically placed ventilation holes, which in fact are knot holes. Where else would you find such a unique solution?

17] Finishing off the cockpit's interior demands a lot of time. Thwarts and lockers are created for specific purposes and are made to fit the shape of the bow.

18] Many finishing touches remain, but the Iversen double-ender looks almost complete. Still to come are the fittings, glazing, pulpit, bow fitting, installation of the motor, and electrical systems, amongst other things.

Virgo

High seas boat

27' 3"	length overall
8' 4"	beam
4.5 long tons	displacement
Volvo Penta MD 22-l, 4-cyl diesel 50 hk	engine
Jac M Iversen	naval architect
Vätö, 1998	place of construction

"Even if you have to push your measuring rule to the limit to create the fastest possible boat, it must still be beautiful, —otherwise you have not succeeded."
Jac M. Iversen

On the care of wooden boats

The subject of proper maintenance of wooden boats generates as many views as there are boat owners. Methods are often a mix of old traditions, new ideas, and the paint manufacturer's technical advise. What works wonders for one boat owner may turn out to be a disaster for someone else—and the result can depend as much on the boat owner as on the product he is using. Part of the fun is finding out what works for you and learning from your experiences.

The manufacturers often have complete paint systems based on one particular primer that needs to be covered by another paint in the same series. It is often a bad idea to mix products from different manufacturers as paints and varnishes are based on different solutions. In the worst case, a varnish from one manufacturer can dissolve the primer from another, which causes cracks and blisters on the surface. But if you are careful and thoroughly follow the instructions, you should avoid such unpleasant surprises. It is also a good idea to ask other experienced yacht people for advice.

The marine carpenter Thomas Larsson has worked on restorations and repairs of wooden boats for 25 years. He has accumulated a thorough knowledge of and experience with different methods. Here is some of his general advice:

- Use the boat for a couple of seasons before you begin renovating, otherwise it is difficult to prioritize the work. Don't start too ambitiously in the fall but plan what you will be able to complete before the next launch. Concentrate on finishing one task properly and ignore the rest. If you do not allow plenty of time for fun on your boat, your passion may wane.

- The wood should to be kept at an even level of moisture all year round. This is what good maintenance of wooden boats is really about. If the boat is properly impregnated and painted, moisture will not have a significant effect on the wood. To completely avoid moisture in a boat is of course impossible but the aim is to keep it out as far as possible. The wood's natural cycle of expansion and shrinkage puts strain on the surface treatment. The bigger the changes, the harder the strain. Hence the boat will be at its best if the keelson is clean and dry. Ensure the keelson is not full of bilge water; use an electric bilge pump with a float switch.

- A covered cockpit makes maintenance easier. The deck and hull have barely any exposed fiber ends and all surfaces are watertight. In comparison the cockpit is full of exposed end pieces and it is also much more difficult to refit. The coverprotects all varnished surfaces.

- The boat needs good ventilation. Try to get as much air as low down in the boat as possible, using a cowl or a solar powered fan. It is a good idea to remove cabin soles and leave hatches open to allow the air to circulate through the whole hull. Good ventilation is the best method for avoiding rot and fungi.

- Store your boat in a roomy boathouse from the fall, around September or October. Air the boat thoroughly until the new year. In January, cover the sides to prevent the spring sun and winds from drying it out. Launch the boat at the end of April or beginning of May. This routine slows down the aging process and keeps maintenance to a minimum.

- In the fall, scrape the bottom of the hull clean where the paint usually peels in springtime. Typically, this is along the garboard strake and the bows. This allows damp patches beneath the paint to dry out which would otherwise cause the wood to crack when the frost comes. Take care when scraping. Other than poor upkeep, too much scraping and frequent changes of ownership represent the biggest threat to a wooden boat. A hull that has been scraped down to its rivets is weakened so much that it is barely possible to salvage.

- Use a long block when you sand large surfaces such as freeboards or the underwater hull. The long block should be made out of plywood as wide as the sanding paper, $\frac{1}{4}$" to $\frac{1}{2}$" thick and 2" to 3" long, with two proper handles attached to the top. Where the hull surface is bent add a layer of soft material —for example a piece of sleeping pad—between the block and the sandpaper to make it more flexible. The long block makes the surface smoother and is easier on the grains.

- The keelson needs a layer of paint that is oil resistant. You don't have to paint the keelson every year, just wash it and paint the patches that need it. Re-painting can lead to too many layers of paint, which sooner or later will peel and cause blisters.

- There is a lot of fashion concerning brands of linseed oil; make sure you use one of high quality. Some linseed oils can cause discoloring on pine. Raw linseed oil is only used for impregnating purposes. It takes a very long time to dry and can be heated into the wood with the help of a hot air fan. Boiled linseed oil is added as a last layer to bind the raw linseed oil.

- "Why are you varnishing when the boat already looks great?" is a common question. Today's varnishes only last one season and the treatment needs to be repeated every year to keep a hardy surface. If you don't sand and varnish the surface, it soon begins to crack and blisters appear: you will have to start again from scratch. To sand and varnish a well-kept wooden boat is easier than washing and treating a plastic hull. But while the plastic boat will allow some degree of neglect, the wooden boat quickly deteriorates and some damage can be impossible to repair.

Glossary

Archer, Colin a famous constructor of Norwegian "sköyter" boats, big Scandinavian double-enders.

ballast weight placed in the keelson to give the boat more stability.

batten down to furl a sail and fasten it.

battens thin, flexible pieces of wood or plastic placed in specially made batten pockets in the leech of the mainsail. Full battens extend all the way from the leech to the luff.

beam reach sailing term for when the wind comes straight at the side of the boat.

beam shelves thick, longitudinal planks, just below deck, for supporting the deck beams.

belay to fasten a rope

belaying pin a short removable iron or wooden pin fitted in a hole in the rail of a boat, used for fastening lines.

belly the shape of the sail. The sail is trimmed for different winds by adjusting the belly.

benar-oil oil for treating wood surfaces, similar to varnish but softer.

bermuda rig a single mast with a beam and a triangular mainsail, as opposed to a gaff rig.

binnacle protective hood over the compass, often artistically made on older boats, using brass plate.

bitt a strong post or bollard for fastening lines; found on deck, usually one of a pair.

bobstay wire or chain stay running from the front of the bowsprit to the head, fastened level with the waterline.

bollard strong metal or wooden pole on a boat for fastening ropes.

boom spar made of wood, fiberglass, or metal, to which sails are attached.

boom tent various types of tents stretched over the cockpit and fastened to the boom.

bowsprit a spar with a fastening for the headsails.

Bruce-anchor modern, effective anchor with three fixed, rounded flukes in the shape of a "duck's foot".

bulkhead an interior wall.

bunk (also berth) a place for sleeping onboard.

burgee wind indicator fitted at the top of the mast.

cabin the coziest and most pleasant place onboard.

cabin sole removable inboard flooring made of wood, metal, or plastic.

caulking a method for making the seams of the planks in a boat's deck or sides watertight; the material itself.

chain plate a fastening for attaching the shroud to the hull.

clinker-built a building technique where the planking timbers for the hull overlap and are fastened to each other with rivets.

clipper a sailboat with clipper bows, ie. an inward pointing bow and a rounded stern with overhang.

cover Waterproof material (eg. canvas) used to cover parts of the boat.

covering board a narrow deck running along the gunwale, all around the boat.

crank instability, the boat sways when the speed increases

cravel-built a construction technique where the planking timbers of the hull are laid flush, edge to edge, and attached only to the frame and floor timbers.

cruiser (eg. skerry cruiser) a boat suitable for longer journeys, with enough room to stay overnight.

deadwood heavy longitudinal timbers fastened over the keelson. The timbers of the bow and stern are fastened to the deadwood.

displacement weight the weight of water that the boat's hull pushes aside, equal to the total weight of the boat.

displacement boat a boat with a keel built for motion,

with a large part of the hull under water.

doghouse large area with glass windows, big enough to stand in, placed between the cabin and the cockpit. Common on motor boats.

dovetail a joint formed by cutting a dovetail shape in one of the two pieces of wood to be joined.

ears the gently curved line of the gunwale between a raised head and a lower plank sheer. The ears are characteristic of Pettersson boats.

fairlead a fitting consisting of two tongues set at an angle, used to keep a rope in place, that forms a part of the ship's rigging and helps avoid chafing.

fenders soft bumper guards that hang along the freeboards to protect the boat from bumps and grazes.

fife rail soft bumper guards, forming a rail around the lower part of a ships mast to which the belaying pins for the rigging are secured.

fin keel a keel that is narrower and deeper than a full keel. Looks like a fish's fin, extending below the boat

floor timber transversal structural member lying across the keel.

flushdeck a deck flush with the hull, without an emphasized gunwale.

Folkboat a clinker-built, one design boat with a transom, designed by Tord Sundén at the beginning of the 1940s. Measures 25' 2" x 7' 3", sail area 260 sq ft.

forecastle a space under the foredeck, fore of the mast.

freeboard the exposed sides of the boat between the gunwale and the waterline.

gaff rig a gaff rig consists of a mast and two booms for the mainsail; the upper boom is called the gaff.

galvanizing to coat iron or steel with a layer of zinc which protects the metal beneath from rust.

garboard plank the first planking, which is attached to the keel timber.

guardwire the safety rail around the gunwale of the boat.

gunwale upper edge of the hull, the border between hull and deck.

halyard rope used for hoisting and lowering a sail.

hand member of the crew.

horn strengthened corner of the sail where halyards or sheets are fastened.

inside planking internal layer of planking, usually composed of wooden strips.

jib triangular staysail set ahead of the foremost mast **keel** lengthways, stabilizing construction under the boat which steadies the course, counteracts sideway lurches and works as a resistance against the wind.

keelson space under the cabin sole, or a long strenghtening timber on top of the keel to add stability to the boat.

king plank a sturdy fore-and aft plank in the middle of the deck, often in a different type of wood.

knee triangular shaped piece of wood used for strenghtening supporting parts of the hull in a wooden boat.

KSSS The Royal Swedish Yacht Club (Kungliga Svenska Segelsällskapet), legendary organization founded in 1830, one of the oldest yacht clubs in the world. KSSS arranges, amongst other things, the ocean race "Gotland Runt".

lateral plane lateral underwater body of the boat, including the keel or centerboard and rudder

Lidingö Yardstick (LYS) a handicap system for sailboats allowing slower boats to compete against faster constructions.

luff (or luff up) to steer the boat closer to the wind.

mainsail the sail on the boom, behind the mast, generally the biggest sail on the boat.

mainsheet traveller track for the sheets of the mainsail.

mälartjugotvåa a fast, Swedish one-design boat, with a sail area of 22 sq m (237 sq ft). Designed in 1929 by Gustaf Estlander with a length of 31 foot and a width of 6 foot. About 100 boats have been built.

mälartrettia entyps segelbåt, Swedish one-design skerry cruiser with a sail area of 30 sq m (322 sq ft) and dimensions of 38' by 6'9". Constructed in 1933 by Lage Eklund. A Mälartrettia is a racing and family boat. About 130 examples were built.

marconi rig an older type of Bermudan rig, often with a rake and a complicated stay. The use of the name Marconi derives from the resemblance to a radio mast, with many stays.

mast heel a heavy piece of timber or a fitting that the mast stands on.

Mejt a famous sailboat owned by the painter Anders Zorn, sometimes used as a floating studio.

MYS Motor Yacht Society, a European organization with the aim of preserving old motor-driven pleasure boats and documenting their history.

oakum yarn of cotton or hemp covered in tar used to caulk the deck or hull.

on the quarters when the wind comes sideways from behind.

one-design boat a boat built strictly according its class rules to be used for competitions with no variation allowed from the detailed hull plans. One-design boats all look the same, as opposed to those designed more freely within a set of rules, such as the R-rule.

Oregon pine high quality pine resembling the heartwood in Swedish pine, used for spars and deck planks.

overhang the parts of the boat's stern and bow which

does not touch the water, common on skerry cruisers.

Owatrol trade name of a petroleum-based oil product used for treating surfaces on wooden boats. The Owatrol system consists of a primer and a varnish which give a glossy finish.

peak 1. the angle between the gaff and mast, important when you raise the sail to prevent the gaff pinching the mast and during sailing to arch the sail. 2. Part of a boat, e.g. forepeak or afterpeak.

Pettersson, C.linG. revolutionary motor boat architect, 1876-1953. Designed the long and narrow Pettersson boat, typified by its straight, raised forebody, often with a cabin, an open cockpit and a sloping transom.

pin rail a rail fastened along the insides of the bulwark of a vessel and pierced to hold belaying pins.

planking longitudinal wooden planks or strakes which form the boat's freeboards.

portlight (or porthole) a small window in a boat.

pre-building term usually used for larger ships, where part of the boats often are

manufactured at another site.

primer dense type of paint applied as a first layer, increases water resistance and works as a bond with the varnish.

quarter sawn a method of planking a log by cutting it into quarters and then creating a series of parallel cuts perpendicular to the tree's rings. This provides an even grain and greater stability but the yield is less than flat sawn lumber.

quarters the sides of the boat astern.

R-yacht a racing yacht constructed according to the universal R-rule, which is an old rule for creating conventionally heavy and powerful racing yachts. Most common among the R-yachts are the 6's, 8's, 10's and 12's.

reach to sail across the wind.

rebate plane a handtool for producing shoulders, grooves, or rebates.

red lead powder lead oxide, poisonous, orange-colored pigment commonly used in wooden boat maintenance. In combination with linseed oil it gives a very dense and hard surface that prevents water from penetrating the wood.

reef to reduce the size of a sail, eg. in strong winds for better sailing.

respond (to the seas) when a boat behaves well on the water.

ribs the "skeleton" of the wooden boat to which the planking is attached.

7/8 rigg common rig type where the forestay is fastened somewhat below the masthead, about $7/8$th of the length of the mast.

Riva exclusive Italian racing boat with amazing finish and an interior resembling an automobile.

rudder post the vertical axle to which the rudder is attached.

run to sail away from the wind.

runabout American term for small open motorboat.

sail-plan a drawing of the various combinations of sails proposed for a sailboat.

Scandinavian double-ender a type of boat originating from the Swedish West Coast which is wide in relation to its length and double-ended with low topsides.

scarph a joint between two wooden pieces, of which

there are many types, eg. keel scarph, hook scarph, lipped scarph.

scull to move the boat forwards with the help of an oar, or the rudder, which is moved forwards and backwards using a certain technique.

seam the narrow gap between the planks which form the decks and sides. Since wood swells when it's in contact with water, a narrow seam is necessary to allow for the expansion.

sheer the curve of the bulkward seen from the side, generally between the head and the sternpost.

sheet a line that controls the angle of the sail in its relation to the wind, which affects the boat's speed.

shelter cabin 1. small cabin to the aft, without a wall. 2. On ships, a small coach roof in front of the companionway.

ship-shape the functional state of the boat when it's tidy, clean, and loose items have been stowed, necessary for the boat to function well in rough weather and tense situations.

sköyte a type of large Norwegian double-ended sailing boat.

sloop a sail boat rigged with one mast and one headsail.

snap on to attach sails to a spar with the help of a rope.

solenoid an electromagnetic coil which causes the axle in a motor to rotate.

spars masts, gaffs, and booms, the load bearing wooden parts of the rig.

splice a join formed from the ends of two pieces of timber or two pieces of rope.

spray hood a small canvas hood in front of the steering position. Protects from wind and splashes and has an aerodynamic effect as the wind is forced up and above.

spreader spars holding the stays away from the mast, which gives a better angle against the mast.

spritsail a square sail with a mast and no boom, where the the sail's outer and upper horn is kept up with a pole—a sprit.

stay a wire between spar and hull which gives strength and stability.

staysail any jib is technically a staysail but the inner jib of a yacht with two jibs is called a staysail, and the outer (foremost) the jib.

steam bending The process of saturating the wood with steam to make it more pliable.

steam box a box or big pipe used to steam the wood during the construction of a boat.

stern the back of the boat.

stem the front and back ends of the boat.

stiff resists heeling, sails upright or returns quickly to the vertical.

tack to turn the bow through the eye of the wind, or the lower forward corner of a triangular sail.

tackle used in combination with a tackle block to ease the necessary weight when, for example, hoisting or trimming a sail.

thwart a seating place in a boat.

tiller lever attached to rudder by which the boat is steered.

topsail the upper sail on aboat with a gaff rig, between gaff and mast.

topping lift the line between the boom end and masthead that prevents the boom from falling when the sail is down.

trunnel wooden peg used instead of a nail. Using old techniques, planking and boards are secured using these small, carved wooden pegs, often made of juniper.

underrigged in regard to sailing boats, having a small sail area in relation to the weight of the hull and stability. These boats are usually slow sailing boats.

vant lateral wire supports for the mast.

Vee-bottom (or hard chine) refers to the bottom of a boat being shaped like a V.

Vega ocean cruiser made from fiberglass, popular one-design boat, constructed by Per Brohäll. About 3,400 were built between 1966 and 1980.

ventilator air vent below deck.

weatherly boat a vessel that tends to move towards the wind.

yacht a sailboat or powerboat used for pleasure not a working boat.

Why choose a wooden boat?

There are many reasons for appreciating wooden boats. As we move towards more eco-friendly times, one reason might be that a wooden boat is made of organic materials which are part of the natural circle of life. Another reason might be the challenge a wooden boat poses to our creative sides, giving us the opportunity to create something beautiful for everyone to enjoy.

A third reason is the fact that a wooden boat gives us the chance to develop positive personal characteristics; work satisfaction, diligence, friendship, pleasure, relaxation, a thirst for knowledge, and a respect for other people.

A fourth reason is the notion that the wooden boat creates its own world. Here, at least, the owner does not have to dance to anyone else's tune.

A fifth and very important reason is the hope that a wooden boat inspires. During winter a wooden boat is on shore, enduring the cold and inhospitable weather. People often loose their spark during the coldest and darkest months, but wooden boats never give up; they help us to look forward.

A sixth reason is the story behind each boat. It is a story told through the marks on the hull, in the cabin sole, or in the planking, which create an atmosphere to reminisce and associate within. A wooden boat is a place for thought; it reminds us of life's conditions, of happiness and disappointment. A wooden boat gives us a perspective on life and ourselves.

Wooden boats carry a heritage, a silent but still vivid heritage. There are some strong imperitives in that heritage, as though the wooden boat was saying: "I'm here! Treat me with respect! You can have me if you want! But it will demand a lot of you! And I'll never be completely yours!"

There are many reasons for appreciating wooden boats, for example...

Sources

Behrens, Björn Peter. *Handbok i träbåtsvård. Renovering och underhåll.*

Nautiska förlaget, 1995.

Biström, Lars, Sundin, Bo. *Svenska båtmotorer.* Båtdokgruppen AB, 1991.

Block, Hanns-Peter. *Ordbok för båtfolk.* Rabén & Sjögren, 1983.

Broch, Ole-Jacob. Träbåten. *Klink, kravell, kaldbaking, reparasjoner*

og vedlikehold. Universitetsforlaget, 1993.

Börjesson, Erik m fl. *Kostern, Segelsällskapet Fram 100 år,* 1996.

Fritz-Crone, G. *C.G. Pettersson – båtkonstruktör och äventyrare.*

Natur och Kultur, 1981.

Hult, Bengt O. *Nautisk uppslagsbok.* Rabén Prisma, 1997.

Larsson, Thomas. Träbåtsrenovering. Series of articles in the magazine

Veteranbåten, 1994.

Motor Yacht Society. Matrikel, 1997.

Speltz, Robert G. *The real runabouts.* 1978.

Storebro – grundat år 1728, 1991.

Thelander, Per. *Alla våra skärgårdskryssare,* 1991.

Ullman, Magnus. *Så levde de.* Bokförlaget Magnus Ullman, 1998.

Östlund, Ruben E. *Motorbåten: konstruktion och bygge.* Bonniers, 1965.

Photography by Ola Husberg with the following exceptions:
From the Fernström family's private collections, p. 13, 15. From the "Segelsällskapet Fram" Picture archive, p. 58. From Björn Kreuger's private collection, p. 66. From the Ljungberg family's private collection p. 67. From the "Svenksa Filminstitutets" picture collection , p 67. From "Dart Industries" catalogue 1931, p. 91. From Storebro Bruks picture archive, p. 114, 115.
Translated by Christopher Ward, Inkwell HB
Graphic design: Bark Design

Skyhorse Publishing books may be purchased in bulk at special discounts for sales promotion, corporate gifts, fund-raising, or educational purposes. Special editions can also be created to specifications. For details, contact the Special Sales Department, Skyhorse Publishing, 307 West 36th Street, 11th Floor, New York, NY 10018 or info@skyhorsepublishing.com.

Skyhorse® and Skyhorse Publishing® are registered trademarks of Skyhorse Publishing, Inc.®, a Delaware corporation.

www.skyhorsepublishing.com

10 9 8 7 6 5 4 3

Library of Congress Cataloging-in-Publication Data is available on file.

ISBN: 978-1-63220-476-9
Ebook ISBN: 978-1-63220-763-0

Cover design by Eric Kang
Cover photos: Ola Husberg

Printed in China